I0024197

Sergei Andreevich Bers, Charles Edward Turner

Recollections of Count Leo Tolstoy

Sergei Andreevich Bers, Charles Edward Turner

Recollections of Count Leo Tolstoy

ISBN/EAN: 9783337319472

Printed in Europe, USA, Canada, Australia, Japan

Cover: Foto ©Thomas Meinert / pixelio.de

More available books at **www.hansebooks.com**

RECOLLECTIONS

OF

COUNT LEO TOLSTOY

TOGETHER WITH

A LETTER TO THE WOMEN OF FRANCE ON
"THE KREUTZER SONATA"

BY

C. A. BEHRS

TRANSLATED FROM THE RUSSIAN BY

CHARLES EDWARD TURNER
ENGLISH LECTURER IN THE UNIVERSITY OF ST. PETERSBURG

LONDON
WILLIAM HEINEMANN
1893

[*All rights reserved*]

CONTENTS.

CHAP.   PAGE

i. INTRODUCTORY 1

ii. BIOGRAPHY OF COUNT TOLSTOY UP TO THE DATE OF
   HIS MARRIAGE 6

iii. FAMILY LIFE OF COUNT TOLSTOY UP TO THE YEAR
   1878 25

iv. CHARACTERISTICS OF COUNT TOLSTOY BEFORE HE
   BEGAN TO TEACH HIS CREED . . . 50

v. MY EXCURSIONS WITH COUNT TOLSTOY AND HIS
   FAMILY 84

vi. COUNT TOLSTOY'S CREED. CHANGE EFFECTED BY IT
   IN HIS PERSONAL CHARACTER. HOW HIS FAMILY
   REGARD HIS TEACHING . 105

A LETTER TO THE WOMEN OF FRANCE ON "THE KREUTZER SONATA."

i. INTRODUCTORY 153

ii. HOW IS THE WOMAN'S QUESTION TO BE SOLVED ? . 165

iii. WHAT IS CHRISTIAN MARRIAGE ? . . . 218

iv. WHAT THEN ARE WE TO DO ? . . 230

RECOLLECTIONS

RECOLLECTIONS

OF

COUNT LEO TOLSTOY.

CHAPTER I.

INTRODUCTORY.

WHEN Count Leo Nicholaevitch Tolstoy began teaching his well-known creed, a general interest was aroused in all that concerned his personal and family life. We all wished to know what kind of life he had led before, how he lived now, and how his family looked upon and regarded his creed.

For the most part all that has hitherto been published on these points is made up of erroneous and fragmentary information, whilst numerous facts have been presented in a false light, and his creed has been put

A *

before the world in a mutilated and distorted shape.

Count L. N. Tolstoy is married to my sister, and from 1866 to 1878 I was accustomed to spend each summer with him and his family, he then being about fifty, and myself a young man of from twenty to twenty-three years of age.

His private life is in every respect irreproachable, and open to the world. All his life he has practised and taught what he believed to be the truth; so that, with perfect justice, he has more than once said to me, " I have nothing to hide from any one in the world : all may know what I do."

Before giving in detail my reminiscences of the Count, I should wish to say a few words concerning our mutual relations.

It will be understood that, then a youth, I not only loved and esteemed him, but accepted him in everything as my guide. Independently of the reverence I felt for his genius, my devoted submission to him

sprang mainly from a rare quality he possessed. A keen psychologist and a skilled
pedagogue, and moreover a man of excep-
tional cordiality and sincerity, he is endowed
with the power of attracting to him not
young men only, but all who are brought
into communication with him, and perhaps
his peculiar gift resides in his rich fund of
marvellous tact and delicacy.

When he was not at work, and of course
in summer he is always comparatively free
and at leisure, I was his constant companion,
and never failed to accompany him on his
journeys or excursions, in his walks, or when
he went shooting.

Like a young enthusiastic disciple, I prized
every minute of his society, and made his
every thought and word my own. Through
the long winter months I lived in the hope
and expectation of being again with him, and,
by corresponding with my sister, kept myself
informed of every little circumstance in their
lives, and was simply in raptures if by chance

he favoured me with a letter from himself, which he did, perhaps, once or twice in the course of the year. In this way I passed my youth and manhood either in the society or under the direct influence of the Count, and I still look back to this period as the best and happiest time in my life.

It was in 1878 that, for the last time, I spent a summer with him, as in that year I commenced my government service in one of the Trans-Caucasian districts.

Since that time I have seen Leo Nicholae-vitch only once, in the autumn of 1887, when I stayed two months with him at Clear Streak-Yásnaya Poliána in the government of Toula.

It was with trembling anticipation that I met my guide and teacher, and, at the end of my two months' visit, he parted coldly from me, since both my life and views were already in discord with his teaching. But even if I had not ceased in my convictions and mode of life to be the zealous follower

of his creed, our once close intimacy must
itself have come to an end.

In my reminiscences of Leo Nicholaevitch
I propose to give a brief biography of the
Count up to the date of his marriage, his
life prior to the above-mentioned year, of
which I was a witness and sharer, and the
impressions produced on me by my last visit,
when the change was already effected in him
which was destined to give an entirely new
direction to his whole intellectual activity,
and a new shape and fashion to the outward
tenor of his life.

CHAPTER II.

*BIOGRAPHY OF COUNT TOLSTOY UP TO THE
DATE OF HIS MARRIAGE.*

COUNT LEO NICHOLAEVITCH TOLSTOY was
born August 28, 1828, on his estate, Clear
Streak-Yásnaya Poliána, in the government
of Toula. The founder of his family, Peter
Andreevitch Tolstoy, was a contemporary
and friend of Peter the Great, who conferred
upon him the title of Count. He was the
descendant of a Prussian emigrant, who later
was appointed ambassador to Turkey, where
he was confined by the Sultan in a seven-
towered castle, whenever any misunderstanding arose between that country and Russia.
It is for this reason that there is a castle on
the coat of arms of the Tolstoy family.

For some generations marriages were concluded between ancestors of Count Leo

Nicholaevitch Tolstoy and princesses who
could boast of direct descent from Rurick.
His mother was Princess Volkonsky, grand-
mother on the paternal side of Princess
Gortshacoff, and of Princess Troubetskoi on
the maternal side. In his personal figure
there is much that recalls his grandfather,
Prince Nicholas Andreevitch Volkonsky, as
may be seen from the portrait of the latter,
drawn at full length in oil-colours. Both
have the same high open forehead, the same
prominent organs of the creative faculty and
of musical talent, the same deep-set grey eyes
that seem to be gazing far into the distance,
and from under the thick overhanging brows
literally pierce the soul of man on whom
they are bent. To such an extent do they
possess this peculiarity that on many they
produce an unpleasing impression. From
the time of his grandfather there has been
preserved a genealogical tree drawn in oil
on linen. The founder of the Volkonsky
family, St. Michael, Prince of Montenegro,

is represented as holding in his hand the
tree, on the branches of which are portraits,
in order of time, of all his descendants.
The likeness the Count and his grandfather
bear to the Montenegrin prince is most
striking, though the painter, of course, could
have had no knowledge of the then unborn
grandson.

The parents of Leo Nicholaevitch made
Clear Streak their principal place of residence, and the life they led, as my grandfather, Alexander Michaelovitch Islenieff,
who was their neighbour and friend, has
told me, was extremely happy, if uneventful.
His father, Count Nicholas Hyine Tolstoy,
served in the Pavlograd regiment of hussars,
and in the campaign of 1812 was made
prisoner by the French. In the novel
"War and Peace" we are introduced to
him under the name of Nicholas Ilyitch
Rostoff, whilst the story of his imprisonment
is described in the chapters relating to the
captivity of Pierre Bezouchoff. I may further

remark that, in his unfinished work, "The
Decembrists," the Count has, in the chapter
entitled, "What kind of Man my Father
was," given us a portrait, not of his father,
but of my grandfather, A. M. Islenieff, with
whom he was intimately acquainted in his
youth.

There is no doubt that, in "War and
Peace," Prince Nicholas Andreevitch Volkonsky and Count Elias Andreevitch Rostoff
are intended to represent the Count's grand-
fathers, Prince Volkonsky and Count Tolstoy,
the novelist having in both cases retained
their real names.   And this is confirmed by
a single glance at their portraits, which are
hanging in the drawing-room of his country
house.

Though Leo Nicholaevitch lost his mother
when he was only three years old, he has
depicted her such as he imagined her to be
in the Princess Marie Volkonsky.   After the
death of his father, when he was nine years
of age, he was, together with his brothers,

all older than himself, and his younger sister, put under the charge, first of his father's sister, Countess Alexandra Ilynina Ostek-Saken, and then of his aunt, Pelgia Ilynina Youschkova, and another of his relations, Tatiana Alexandrevna Eyelskaya, both of whom died in his house at a ripe old age during one of my visits to Yásnaya Poliána.

Yásnaya Poliána, the ancestral estate of the Volkonskys, is situated close to the crossing-point of three roads, the Moscow-Kursk railway, the Toula-Kieff highway, and the old Toula-Krapievinsk road, at about fifteen versts' distance from Toula. Its name, Clear Streak, sufficiently evidences the lively picturesqueness of its site. Somewhat hilly, it is surrounded on all sides by an immense forest, that belongs to the imperial domains, and is called Zaseika. The estate, with its fine avenues of old lime-trees, that were planted by the Count's great-grandfather, its four ponds, and wild uncultivated grounds, is shut in by a castellated rampart, whose lofty brick towers frown down on the road near the entrance gates. These three towers, as old folks relate, were in the time of the Count's grandfather, who held the rank of general under Paul the First, constantly guarded by sentries.

According to the testimony of Leo Nicholaevitch's aunt, P. I. Youschkova, he was as a child excessively frolicsome and playful, and in his boyhood was distinguished by a strange propensity for doing things the least expected and most eccentric, being in character as lively as he was generous and warm-hearted.

It was the same aunt who related to me how once, being on a journey with posthorses, they had already taken their places in the carriage, when the boy was nowhere to be found, and they began to search and call for him. A minute later his head was pushed out of the window of the little poststation, as he cried, " Ma tante, I will come directly." Half of his head was seen to be closely shaved. The fancy had taken him, for some reason or other, to get his hair clean cut during the short time in which fresh horses were being put to.

My mother has told me that, in the description he gives of his first love in his earliest story, "Childhood," the Count omits to relate how, on one occasion, impelled by jealousy, he angrily pushed the object of his affection, who was no other than herself, then in her ninth year, from off the balcony. This outburst of rage was due to the fact that she dared to talk with others, instead of reserving her attentions exclusively to himself.

Leo Nicholaevitch received his first education at home, and then entered the Kazan University, which at that time enjoyed considerable favour among the Russians, and where his three brothers had taken their degrees. Like most of our great writers and geniuses, he did not finish his university studies, and only concluded his third course in the faculty of Oriental Languages, having previously been entered in the Mathematical, Medicinal, and Law faculties. His failure at the university, to judge from what he has often told me, would seem to have been a source of great annoyance and disappointment to him. But it may be attributed to his want of steady application to any particular branch of study, and his unwillingness to remain permanently on one and the same faculty. In spite of his failure, however, he later, between the years 1870 and 1880, was elected honorary member of the Academy of the Sciences, a distinction conferred upon him in recognition of the high merits of his dissertation on the national war of 1812, a subject that always interested him, and which he subsequently selected for the theme of his great work, "War and Peace."

Nor was this by any means the only disappointment Leo Nicholaevitch experienced in his youth. But none the less he kept constantly before him the desire to perfect his nature, to obtain a complete mastery over himself, and to achieve all that is good, just, honourable, and pure. He was urged to this moral struggle by the consciousness of his impulsive and passionate temperament. Even as a boy he began to note down with scrupulous accuracy, in a copy-book specially reserved for that purpose, every little sin he had committed since his last confession, in order that he might repent such sins, and, if possible, refrain from fresh relapses, and particularly from any offence against the seventh commandment.

Being the youngest of the brothers, he would seem to have been most attached to Nicholas Nicholaevitch, the eldest. The latter died many years ago, and his bust in marble may be seen in the Count's study at Yásnaya Poliána. He also possessed no ordinary talents, but was carried off by consumption just when he was beginning his literary career. Two or three of his productions appeared in the pages of the *Contemporary*. He was as kind-hearted as he was strangely absent-minded. On one occasion he forgot to put on his student's uniform, and appeared in the university lecture-room in his dressing-gown. Tourgenieff once said of him that he possessed all the merits and none of the shortcomings of a good writer. He warmly returned his younger brother's affection, and throughout his life exercised on him a beneficial influence. He served in the artillery in the Caucasus during the war with the mountain tribes, and persuaded Leo Nicholaevitch, when he quitted the university, to join the army; and he accordingly set off with his brother to the Caucasus as a non-commissioned officer.

In a *tarantass*, or travelling-coach, accompanied by one servant, they set out from Kazan and made their way along the left bank of the Volga. But they soon grew tired of journeying in a coach, and, having secured a large barge, put the *tarantass* into it; and, letting themselves float down with the current, passed the days very pleasantly in reading and enjoying the scenery. Their voyage extended over three weeks, but at last they arrived at Astrachan. More than once, as they drew to shore in the lower flats of the Volga, they came across half-savage Calmucks grouped around huge piles of blazing wood, the larger number of the Calmucks being at that time still fire-worshippers.

Leo Nicholaevitch was always very fond of talking over his experiences in the Caucasus. Its rich and glorious scenery, the magnificent sport it afforded, and the repeated skirmishes in which he was engaged with the mountaineers, all this delighted and inspired the young writer. It was there, in his twenty-third year, that he wrote his first tales, "Childhood, Boyhood, and Youth."

It was also in the Caucasus that he met with the following adventure, which forms the subject of his story, "The Caucasian Prisoner."

A certain Sodó, of the tribe of the Tchetchenians, and with whom the Count was on friendly terms, had bought a young horse, and one day proposed to him to take a ride into the country surrounding the fortress, where the detachment of the Russian army in which he then served was posted. Two other officers of the artillery joined the party. Though all such excursions had been strictly forbidden by the military authorities in consequence of the serious dangers with which they were accompanied, not one of them, except Sodó, was furnished with any other weapon than the ordinary Circassian sabre. Having tried his own horse, Sodó begged his friend to mount it, and himself leaped on the Count's trotter, which, of course, was no good at a fast gallop. They were already about five versts from the fortress when suddenly they saw close before them a band of Tchetchenians, some twenty in number. The Tchetchenians began to pull their guns from their covers, and divided themselves into two parties. One half of them set off in chase of the two officers, who were already making what speed they could back to the fortress, and soon overtook them. One of the officers was pulled from his horse and hacked to pieces; the other was taken prisoner. Sodó, followed by Leo Nicholae-vitch, pushed off in another direction towards a Cossack picket that was posted at about a verst distant. Their pursuers were close upon them, and there was nothing before them but death or captivity, with its usual accompaniment, to be put into a pit neck high and left there to starve, for the moun-taineers were noted for their cruel treatment of the unlucky wretches who fell into their hands. It was possible for Leo Nicholae-vitch to escape on his friend's swift-footed steed, but he would not abandon him. Sodó, like a true mountaineer, had not failed to bring his gun with him, but unfortunately it was unloaded. He none the less aimed at his pursuers, and with a wild cry of defiance made as if he were on the point of firing.

To judge from what followed, we may
presume that it was their intention to take
them both prisoners, in order that they might
better revenge themselves on Sodó. At any
rate, they none of them fired. It was this
alone that saved their lives. They managed
to get within sight of the picket, whence the
sharp-eyed sentry had from a distance seen
the danger they were in, and instantly gave
the alarm. The Cossacks soon turned out,
and before long compelled the Tchetchenians
to cease their pursuit.

Sodó's love for his Russian friend was unselfish and sincere. On another occasion he
rendered a service of no little value to his
koumák—the word which, in the language of
his tribe, signifies friend.

Leo Nicholaevitch had played at cards
and lost heavily. There was no possibility
of discharging his debt within the appointed
time, since he had been disappointed in the
receipt of some money he expected from
home. His position was by no means an

enviable one. That Count Tolstoy, the rich junker, should fail to pay a card-debt with all due punctuality was, as we may suppose, deeply wounding to his self-love, and likely to lower him in the opinion of his fellow-officers. In his despair, he shut himself up in his room, and prayed to God that He would save him from this disgrace. His prayer was interrupted by the delivery of a letter from Sodó. He opened the envelope and found in it the torn pieces of his note-at-hand. He afterwards learned that Sodó had that day won a large sum at cards, and had made use of his winnings to pay the debt his friend had incurred.

I may remark that the custom of making presents is far more widely spread, and has a stamp of greater sincerity, in the East than with us in Europe. Our ideas of politeness and self-respect frequently induce us to decline the receipt of a present, whilst any such refusal is regarded by Orientals as a serious and intentional insult.

In recompense for his service in the
Caucasus, Leo Nicholaevitch was very
anxious to receive the Cross of St. George,
and he was even recommended for it, but did
not obtain it in consequence of the personal
ill-feeling entertained towards him by one
of his superior officers. He was naturally
vexed, but the disappointment served to
change his ideas of true bravery. He
ceased to count those as brave who achieve
some rare act of boldness on the battlefield,
and thereby obtain a high rank or distinguished order. The man who does not fail
to preserve his reason, and act accordingly
in the presence of danger henceforth formed
his ideal of real courage. This view he
has taken care to insist on in several of
his works. Thus, in "The Raid," the
simple-minded Captain Chlopoff is put
forth as the true hero, and in "War and
Peace" the modest Captain Touschine is
represented as the type of real courage.

During the Crimean campaign Leo Nichol-

aevitch was on active service, first under
Silistria, and, after the siege of that fortress
was raised, at Sevastopol, where, it may be
mentioned, in the fourth bastion, he was
under fire for three days.

Whilst he was at Sevastopol he was a
constant visitor at the house of his near
relation, Prince Gortshacoff, Commander-in-
Chief of the Russian forces; but he de-
clined an appointment on the staff that was
offered him, and continued serving in the
ranks of the army. The reason for his
preference for this service he has himself
explained in those portions of his works
where he contends that the influence exercised by the staff with its plans on the
conduct of a war is invariably pernicious.

It was at this time he composed his
famous song, "The Eighth of September,"
which was sung not only in his own regiment,
but was caught up and became popular
among the soldiers of the whole army.

Wherever he went he was always ac-

companied by his serf Alexis, whom he
has introduced into several of his novels
under the name of Aloscha.   At Sevastopol.
it was Alexis who carried the rations to
the bastion, a duty that frequently exposed
him to serious danger.   I have often seen
this Alexis after he was appointed steward
of the estate at Yásnaya Poliána.   He was
younger than his master, to whom he was
passionately devoted.   Reserved and silent
by nature, I have never known him to give
any interesting details of the life and
military service of his master.

After the Crimean War Leo Nicholaevitch quitted the army with the rank of
lieutenant in the artillery.   The period in-
tervening between his quitting the military
service and his marriage was spent partly
at St. Petersburg, partly abroad, and partly
in the steppes of Bashkir, where he went
to drink koumiss.

He had always an inveterate dislike for
St. Petersburg.   He could never be at his

ease in the so-called high society of the
capital; he did not care to enter the civil
service; he did not possess any very large
fortune, and had not as yet made for himself
a name in literature, since his two best
works, "War and Peace" and "Anna
Karénina," were still unwritten. He remained in St. Petersburg a little over six
months. Whilst abroad, he chiefly interested himself in studying the question
of education for the people, and in visiting
different schools. He had always a strong
preference for country life, and, accordingly,
on his return from the Continent, made
Yásnaya Poliána his habitual place of residence, and devoted himself to literary
occupations and to the school he established
there.

CHAPTER III.

A VERY slight acquaintance with the works of Count Tolstoy is sufficient to show how highly he rates the happiness of family life. According to his own confession to have a home of his own was the dream of his youth.

His marriage took place on September 23, 1862, when he was already thirty-four years of age, his wife being then in her eighteenth year.

He had long been on the most intimate terms with our family, having known my mother from her childhood.

My late father had no liking for our educational institutes and gymnasiums for girls, and my sister was therefore educated and brought up at home; but she went up for the examination at the university, and obtained the diploma giving her the rights of a private governess. During the whole of her girlhood she kept a diary, and not seldom tried her hand at writing tales and novels, but chiefly showed a special talent for painting.

How he sought and obtained her hand in marriage he has described to us, with accurate fidelity to the minutest detail, in his "Anna Karénina," in the chapter where Levine and Kate make use of the initial letters of the words in which they wish to express to each other their mutual love.

From people who knew nothing of my relationship with the Count, I have heard it suggested, when the conversation happened to turn on "The Kreutzer Sonata," that, in all probability, Leo Nicholaevitch himself had gone through the experiences of Poduiescheff, and thus the mere fantasies natural to great talent and genius formed the ground of his false suspicions of his wife.

I may, perhaps, be allowed to speak with authority on this point, since there is no one who has been a closer witness of their family life than myself during my long and frequent visits to Yásnaya Poliána; but it ought to be sufficient to recall the fact that my father and mother, who, like all parents, were disposed to be discontented with the lot of their children, would often exclaim, "In our wildest dreams we have never desired greater happiness for our daughter."

And throughout her whole married life his wife has never failed in deep admiration for him as writer, and in equally deep love for him as husband.

And on his side, Leo Nicholaevitch has often said that he has found in his family life the completest happiness, and in her not only an affectionate wife and perfect mother, but a help and an aid in his literary career. We may also notice that in his written thoughts, ideas, and sentiments he constantly renders her every warm and loving eulogy.

As both possess in a high degree a straight-forwardness and frankness of character, I have often fancied that each is aware of what the other may be thinking of at any given moment. But there is no need to dwell on their mutual relations. These are plain and evident, even to any stranger who may chance to see them together.

As his help and aid in all his literary labours, she has well merited the gratitude of posterity.

In her conduct and bearing towards her husband and his literary productions, she always reminds me of a religious worshipper and zealous guardian of some sacred well. Her self-imposed task, owing to his careless-ness and those unmethodical habits which seem to be common to all geniuses, has never been an easy one. In proof of this I may state that the composition of his novel "War and Peace" began immediately after their marriage, and extended over a period of eight years. During that time, in

addition to all her occupations as mother of
the four children who were born in the in-
terval, she copied out the romance no less
than seven times.

It was she who always collected and put
into order the scraps and bits of papers on
which he is wont to write his works. She
only is able to make out with comparative
ease his marvellously illegible handwriting,
to decipher his hastily scratched scrawls and
fantastic hieroglyphics, and to guess correctly
from his incompleted words and phrases,
which he had either not the time or the
patience to finish, the ideas and thoughts he
wished to express. Her faultless capacity
in this respect is a frequent theme of the
Count's astonishment and praise.

Nor should I forget to remark that she
has, with laudable accuracy and care, copied
out and preserved all the manuscripts of
those of his works which have never been
published.

I remember how, simultaneously with all

this literary work, and all her household cares, she still found time to suckle, and later to teach and make clothes for, all her children up to their tenth year.

At the actual moment, the children of Leo Nicholaevitch are nine in number, the eldest being twenty-eight and the youngest three years of age.

With the exception of the second daughter, all the children were suckled by the mother, from which we perceive that, even before the Count had made this a cardinal point in his social creed, hired wet-nurses were not admitted into his house.

I recollect how, after the birth of the second daughter, the Count's wife, through the carelessness of one of the servants, fell dangerously ill, and it was necessary to have recourse to the services of a wet-nurse. But when the poor mother saw her child sucking a stranger's breast, she burst into a torrent of jealous tears, and then and there dismissed the nurse, and ordered the child to be fed

with a bottle. When Leo Nicholaevitch
was told of what had happened, he said
that she had only shown the jealous affection
of a true mother for her child.

I shall now pass on to the system of
education practised by the Count in relation
to his children, long before he had published
any of his numerous essays and articles on
this subject.

Everything that concerned, however re-
motely, the bringing up and instruction of
his children was under his immediate direction, and the wife willingly confined herself
to a faithful and obedient execution of his
instructions and wishes.

His views on education were based for the
most part on the teaching of Jean Jacques
Rousseau. And if he did not carry out to
their fullest extent the ideas advocated in
" Emile," this was only because his wife
was unable to act upon them in every case,
and he himself was too occupied with his
literary labours.

As we have seen, he counselled his wife
to suckle her children, and not to intrust
them to wet-nurses. In this she completely
sympathised with him. Toys and playthings
were rigorously banished from the nursery.
With the first child the trial was made to
dispense altogether with a nurse. But later
it was thought well to yield to the requirements of their social position and to the
habits of contemporary life, and the children
were put under the care of nurses, bonnes,
and governesses. The parents, however,
invariably exercised a strict and unremittent
surveillance over both the children and those
who had the care of them.

The greatest possible liberty was allowed
to the children, and all put in authority over
them were strictly forbidden to have resort
under any pretext to violent or severe punish-
ments.

Leo Nicholaevitch believed that these
principles were nowhere so generally accepted as in England; and, accordingly,

from their third to their ninth year, the children were placed under the charge of young English governesses, engaged directly from London.

They were extremely fortunate and happy in their first choice. Their first English governess remained with them for above six years, and, when she had resigned her duties, continued to be, and still is, in most friendly relations with the family.

The one aim to which the governesses constantly devoted themselves was to make the children well acquainted with everything in nature, and to inspire them with a love, unmingled with fear, for all natural objects, animals, and insects.

Leo Nicholaevitch liked to impress on a child the consciousness of its powerlessness in the presence of nature, and its dependence on its elders, but, whilst discovering to it the truth, he strictly refrained from inspiring it with fear or dread.

When the children required the servants

C

to do anything, they were forbidden to be peremptory and were required to *ask* that a thing should be done.   And that the necessary example might be set them, all in the house were expected to do the same.

Independently of sympathy for their fellow-creatures, a like feeling for all animals was sedulously cultured.

A lie was never passed over.   The punishment, however, did not consist in the actual infliction of pain or shame, such as confinement of the offender to his room, but simply in the withdrawal on the part of the parents of all interest in or care for anything the child said or did.   Directly the child showed genuine sorrow for what it had done, the punishment was revoked.

But the children were never allowed to get off by a mere promise that the offence should not be repeated, or by simply praying for pardon.

A full and frank confidence in their parents was thus cultivated by just and

kindly treatment.   It was they, and they
alone, who, when necessary, were permitted
to inflict a punishment.

All in the house were made to understand
that children are always disposed to copy
and imitate what they see or hear.   They
were, therefore, never allowed to be alone
or to mix in any society, but were constantly
in the company of the grown-up members
of the household ; and for this reason, perhaps, when eight o'clock struck, the hour for
them to go to bed, Leo Nicholaevitch would
at times give a sigh of relief and exclaim,
" Well, at last we are free ! "

The elementary lessons in Russian and in
music were given by the mother, whilst those
in arithmetic were given by Leo Nicholaevitch himself.

For the foreign languages, besides the
English governess there were engaged at
different times during my visits to their house
a Swiss, a Frenchman, a German, and a
Swiss lady.   Tutors and students, who were

also lodged at Yásnaya Poliána, taught the other subjects. For the music lessons a master came over from Toula. After his pupils had practised the finger exercises, the Count insisted on their proceeding at once to learn serious pieces, under which term he did not include operas. Lessons in painting were given only to those of the children who showed a real capacity for it ; though from their earliest years every effort was made to foster and develop such talent.

The theory that no compulsion should be exercised on a pupil, and that full liberty should be accorded him in the choice of subjects to be studied, of which Leo Nicholaevitch is so stanch a partisan in his educational articles, was adopted only to a certain extent. In practice, the universal application of this principle was found to be inconvenient and even impossible.

Notwithstanding his contempt and dislike for the programme of studies adopted in our gymnasiums, the Count did not consider

himself justified in depriving his sons of the
possibility of entering the university. He,
therefore, made them follow these pro-
grammes. His eldest son each year passed
his examination together with the other students at the Toula Classical Gymnasium.
In this way he was prepared at home for the
university, which he entered in his eighteenth
year.

The children were never punished for
having neglected to prepare their lessons,
or for repeating them badly, but were rewarded whenever they had learned well.

These concessions in respect to the subject
of study being made compulsory, and the
engagement of strange tutors and masters,
were made in deference to the prevailing
rule and views of the social circle in which
his children would later have to move.

After the conclusion of the marriage
ceremony, the Count with his wife set off
for Yásnaya Poliána. From that time up to
the year 1880 they lived there constantly

winter and summer, with the exception of two summers, which they spent on his estate in the government of Samara, and a few months one winter, which they passed at Moscow, where our family constantly resided.

Leo Nicholaevitch has been his whole life, in the strict sense of the word, a hard worker. In nearly every letter I received from my sister I find the words, "We are all very busy. The winter is our busiest time." It was chiefly during the winter months that Leo Nicholaevitch wrote, often a whole day at a sitting and late into the night. It would seem that he never waited, or acknowledged the wisdom of waiting, for inspiration. Every morning he would take his place before his desk and begin to work. If he did not write anything, he was busy making extracts and collecting materials for the book on which he happened to be engaged. Generally at dinner, before resuming work, he would read an English novel. Even in the summer, when the children

were having their holidays and his wife
would beg him to take a rest, it was not
always that he consented. I have never
discovered, even in the most conscientious
of men, such a strict and persistent devotion
to work as characterised Leo Nicholaevitch.

In the morning he used to come and
dress in his study, where a bed was put
up for me immediately under an engraved
portrait of the great Schopenhauer. Before
breakfast we either went out for a walk
together or took a ride to the baths. The
breakfast hour was the pleasantest and least
constrained time in the whole day at Yásnaya Poliána. Then the whole family was
assembled. The conversation was always
lively, and rendered all the gayer by the
Count's jokes and quips, and by the different
proposals as to how the day should be spent.
And the chatting usually went on till Leo
Nicholaevitch got up with the words, " It
is time to work now," and went into his

room, carrying with him a glass of strong tea.

As long as he was occupied in his room, no one dared to enter or interrupt him. Even his wife had not boldness enough to think of such a thing. It is true that at one time his eldest daughter, then a mere child, was privileged to set the rule at defiance.

To tell the truth, no one could welcome more heartily than I did the days when it chanced that he did not work, since in his free time we were always together.

The circle of his acquaintances, as distinct from relatives and friends, was extremely limited.

Of his nearer relations, my younger sister with her family spent regularly every summer with him and his people. She is portrayed in his novel "War and Peace" in the person of Natasha Rostoff, and nearly all her youth was passed at Yásnaya Poliána.

Among his friends who frequently visited him may be mentioned N. Strachoff, well

known for his able and appreciative criticisms
of Count Tolstoi's principal productions,
who seldom let a summer go by without
coming to see him; D. Diakoff, who had
known him from his boyhood; and Prince
Ouronsoff, the mathematician. These make
up the list of those who were then on terms
of friendship with Leo Nicholaevitch.

I may be expected here to say a few
words concerning the relation in which he
stood towards Ivan Sergeivitch Tourgenieff.
When his stories "Childhood and Youth"
first appeared, Tourgenieff was one of the
earliest to recognise their rare merits, and to
predict a great future for their author. A
friendship soon sprang up between the two
writers; but, for reasons with which I am
unacquainted, their friendship gradually
cooled into something like enmity and
aversion. Subsequently they again became
reconciled, and in the summer of 1874
Tourgenieff came over to Yásnaya Poliána
and spent a day there. I accompanied

Leo Nicholaevitch to Toula, where he met his literary rival and fellow-artist. At dinner Tourgenieff talked much, and to the delight of the younger folks not only mimicked several persons of whom he was speaking, but imitated different animals. Thus, by a cunning manipulation of his fingers, he made the figure of a fowl waddling in the soup, and further gave an admirable imitation of a hunting-dog at loss. As I listened to him and watched his tricks I couldn't help thinking that he evidently inherited something of the talent for which one of his ancestors under Peter the Great enjoyed no little fame.

The acquaintances of the Count visited Yásnaya Poliána very seldom.

The secluded life which he led may be explained by a natural disinclination to be hampered and interrupted in the literary work that occupied so much of his time by the ceremonious entertainments that necessarily accompany the reception of visitors. His

large family, and the number of relatives
who made it a rule to spend each summer
at Yásnaya Poliána rendered it both unnecessary and troublesome to receive
visitors.

The children were only too glad to be
in his company, and each was eager to
play on his side; and they were never
more happy than when he taught them a
new game.   Under his winning influence
and good humour they willingly and without
difficulty would go with him on foot to
Toula, a distance of at least fifteen versts.
The boys with gleeful pride and an utter
unconsciousness of fatigue accompanied him
when he went out shooting with his dogs.
There was no occasion for him to call
them a second time when he took them
to practise gymnastics, or to play at some
game, in which he showed as keen and
eager an interest as they did themselves.
In winter they often went skating with
him, but their greatest pleasure was when

he invited them to help him in clearing
the snow from the skating-rink. Although
he himself never went mushrooming, a
favourite amusement at Yásnaya Poliána,
he encouraged others to do so. With me,
he liked to mow the lawn, to rake the
garden-beds, to practise gymnastics, to have
a running race, or a good game at leap-
frog or skittles. Though he was greatly
my superior in physical strength, for he
could lift with one hand a weight of 120
lbs., I could very easily beat him in a
running match, but seldom succeeded in
passing him, since, just as I was preparing
to make the necessary spurt, he would say
or do something that forced me to stop
from laughing. If, as sometimes happened
in our walk, we came across a group of
mowers, he liked to take the scythe from
the labourer who seemed to be most tired,
and would let him rest whilst he himself
worked. On such occasions he has more
than once asked me how it comes that, in

spite of our well-developed muscles, we cannot mow for six days running, whilst a common peasant who sleeps on the damp ground and lives on black bread can easily do it. And he generally wound up the subject by exclaiming, "You just try it and see!" And as he left the meadow he would pluck from the ricks a tuft of hay and literally revel in its fragrant smell.

I have spoken of Count Tolstoy's humour, which was of an extremely varied kind. In citing a few examples, I fear much that what amused us will appear tame to the general reader, who must necessarily remain ignorant of the trifling incident that gave them point and provoked our hearty laughter.

All the members of our family are delicately built, and therefore none of us like to sit on hard seats. One of my younger brothers thought it necessary to explain to us that he should take some soda, as he had bile on the stomach. Leo Nicholaevitch broke into a loud laugh, and counselled him to take a good walk of twenty versts, and afterwards, if any of us complained of any little inconvenience or discomfort, would cry out, "Ah, you have got Boris's bile, and cannot sit quiet." When Leo Nicholaevitch wished to refrain from an extra cigar or from a second helping to a favourite dish, he consoled himself by saying, "Wait till I am grown up, and then I will have two helpings to that dish;" or, "Will smoke two cigars." Once my sister was getting ready to go to town and make some purchases, and, before starting, consulted with him as to what dresses she should buy for the children and herself, whereupon he replied, "There is business cut out for four hundred linen-drapers." If ever he proposed an excursion he would, before deciding on it, add, "But we must first hear what our prime-minister has to say to it," by which term he meant his wife, without whose advice and approval he never allowed anything to be done. If he noticed any of the children making a wry or affected face, he generally called out, " Now, then, no grimacing, you will only spoil your phiz." Leo Nicholaevitch was very fond of playing duets with his sister, Marie Nicholaevna. But the Countess was an admirable musician, and to keep up with her through a long piece was no easy task. He would, when in difficulty, say something to make her laugh, which caused her to play a little slower, and gave him time to catch her up. And if that did not answer, he would stop and solemnly take off one of his boots, as if that must help him, and then go on, as he exclaimed, " Now, it will go all right !" But what he called " the Numidian cavalry charge" invariably evoked our noisiest applause. It consisted in his suddenly springing up from his place and, with one hand raised in the air and the other grasping an imaginary bridle, commencing a wild gallop round the room, in which the children, and not seldom we elder ones, liked to join. He was a good reader, and often read aloud to us. I still remember his reading one evening Gogol's "Story of Captain Kopeikine."

And so Leo Nicholaevitch's family life was too full and complete to leave him a care for distraction and amusement elsewhere, beyond his own circle. And if he were only with us, we required no other company. Nor was this feeling peculiar to myself or to be attributed to my youthfulness. It was shared by everbody, young or old, who had the good fortune to be with him.

After my last visit, before I left for my new post in one of the Trans-Caucasian districts, to judge from the letters I received from my sister and her children, who were then grown up, their circle of acquaintances began to grow wider and wider, and from the year 1880 they regularly spent each winter in Moscow.

For himself, he never cared to leave his family for however short a time. When it

was absolutely necessary for him to go to
Moscow, either to superintend the publication of his newest work or to engage a tutor
for his children, he used to grumble long
and terribly over his hard fate. And when
he came within sight of his home, as he·
returned from a journey or from shooting, he would often express his anxiety by
exclaiming, "I only hope all is well at
home!" On such occasions he never failed
to amuse and interest us with long accounts
of what he had seen and heard.

CHAPTER IV.

CHARACTERISTICS OF COUNT TOLSTOY BEFORE HE BEGAN TO TEACH HIS CREED.

IF we would form a just estimate of the peculiar traits in the character and teaching of Leo Nicholaevitch, we must not forget the close relation they have to the views and opinions of Jean Jacques Rousseau. There is no doubt that the writings of the French thinker had a great influence on his own mode of thought. He was still young when he first became acquainted with them, and was immediately attracted by them.

In their love of nature, and in their preference for all that is simple, coupled with a strong aversion to modern civilisation, we recognise the salient points of

resemblance that have been wont, and still
continue to characterise these two writers.
A hundred years have passed, and Rousseau
still speaks in the pages of our Russian
Tolstoi.

Most of us, if we remark the beauties
of nature, are rarely, if ever, moved to
raptures over them. It was not so with
Leo Nicholaevitch. Every day of his
life he showed and expressed his joyous
recognition of her charms. "What inex-
haustible wealth is enjoyed by God! Each
new day reveals to Him some fresh beauty,
distinguishing it from all that have gone
before."

In his works we read that the agriculturist
and sportsman alone know nature; and he
himself was a keen sportsman, and still is an
agriculturist.

No bad weather was allowed to interfere
with his daily walk. He could put up with
loss of appetite, from which he occasionally
suffered, but he could never go a day without

a sharp walk in the pure open air. In general, he was fond of active movement, riding, gymnastics, but particularly walking. If his literary work chanced to go badly, or if he wished to throw off the effects of any unpleasantness, a long walk was his sovereign remedy. He could walk the whole day without feeling fatigued; and we have often ridden for ten or twelve hours. In his study he kept a pair of dumb-bells, and would often busy himself with putting up or repairing gymnastic appliances.

His aversion to modern civilisation is mainly shown in his dislike of cities and city life. He made his stay in any town as short as possible, and lived almost uninterruptedly in the country, where, he declared, man alone can live. When he happened to be with me in St. Petersburg or Moscow, I noticed how, almost with our arrival, a fit of dulness came over him, and how he grew fidgety and even irritable.

In his dislike of anything like luxury in

the ordering of his house and surroundings he denied the reasonableness or charm of comfort, whose influence he believed to be prejudicial to the souls and bodies of men. Nothing could be more simple than the arrangement of his house at Yásnaya Poliána.

He was in no wise fastidious or particular as to what he ate, could not sleep on a spring-mattress, did not like a soft bed, and at one time always slept on a leather-covered sofa.

He dressed extremely simply, and when at home never wore starched shirts, or what our peasants call German clothes. His costume consisted of a grey flannel blouse, which in summer he exchanged for a canvas one, of a very original cut, as we judge from the fact that there was in the whole district only one old woman, a certain Barbara, who could make it according to his orders. In this blouse Leo Nicholaevitch has sat for his portrait to Kramsky and

Repine, the painters. His over-dress was composed of a caftan and half-shouba, made of the simplest materials, and, like the blouse, eccentric in their cut, being made evidently not for show but to stand bad weather. For the latter reason, doubtless, they were often borrowed and made use of by his home-people or guests.

In spite, however, of his simple dress, he preserved in it his striking and original look. Kramsky several times expressed a wish to paint a portrait of him in his caftan on horseback.

Leo Nicholaevitch could never bear railroads. His dislike for them he has over and over again expressed in his different works. He complained of the disagreeable sensations he experienced in a railway carriage. He stoutly maintained, as indeed he does in his "Educational Papers" for 1862, that they had brought no good or benefit to the people at large, and could not tolerate either the officious politeness of the conductor or the way in which passengers suspiciously shunned one another. Contrary to the majority of men, he liked few things better than to get into chat with any chance fellow-passenger. He preferred to travel by third class, and constantly chose the carriage in which there happened to be most moujiks.

He further resembled Rousseau in his opinion and estimate of doctors and medicine. In both "War and Peace" and in "Anna Karénina" he indulges in a merciless attack on the doctors who were called in to attend Natasha Rostoff and Katie Scherbatoff, declaring that, like all doctors, they were completely ignorant of the causes or right treatment of human maladies. Like Rousseau, he held that the practice of medicine should be made general and not confined to one profession. Hence his preference for popular medicines and for midwife remedies. None the less, when there was illness in his family, he called in and consulted Professor Zacharine, and one summer himself went through a course of mineral waters.

Once more, like Rousseau, Leo Nicholae-vitch has won to himself considerable fame as a talented pedagogue.

I myself have proved his large-minded experience as a pedagogue. I remember how he never shirked discussing with me and explaining any difficulty I might have encountered in my scientific or philosophical studies, never seeming to think it was a condescension on his part to talk on such subjects with an unripe youth. To all my questions his answers were simple, clear, and to the point. Nor was he ashamed, when necessary, to confess his ignorance and to declare "Well, you see, I do not quite understand that myself." At times, our conversation assumed the shape of a debate, in which I was always permitted to speak out frankly, though I was never uncon-scious of my incomplete knowledge in com-

parison with his wide grasp of nearly every
subject on which I had occasion to consult
him. All this made it easy and pleasant
to me to agree with him, and to accept implicitly his views and opinions.

Leo Nicolaevitch was always fond of
children, and liked to have them around
him. He easily wor their confidence, and
seemed to have found the key to their
hearts. He appeared to have no difficulty
in suiting himself to a strange child, and
with his first question set it completely at
ease, so that it began at once to chat away
with perfect freedom. Independently of
this, he divined with all the skill of a
trained pedagogue the thoughts of a child.
I remember his children one day ran up
to him, and told him they had a great
secret, and when they persisted in refusing
to divulge it, he quietly whispered in their
ears what it was. "Ah, what a papa ours
is! How did he find it out?" they cried,
in a chorus of bewilderment.

In his " Educational Papers " for 1862, he attacks the system, which by the way obtains everywhere, of forcing a scholar to study according to a fixed programme of subjects. Every one who has read the article entitled " Yásnayà Poliána School in November and December, 1862," will understand that the principle of liberty in the choice of studies was fully carried out and acted upon in this school. It must be remembered by the opponents of this theory that in the school were peasant children who, scarcely able to write, soon learned to compose short tales and stories in prose. None but a practised pedagogue could have succeeded, with these unpromising materials, in effecting such progress.

Count Tolstoy's educational activity dates from the time when he began to teach his own children. This was soon after he had finished his romance, " War and Peace." It was then he wrote his " Alphabet Book," his "Tales for Children," and his "Manual of Arithmetic."

His educational theories have a close connection with, and explain his relation to, the peasantry.

He may with truth claim to himself the title of the friend of the Russian people. From his earliest years he knew and loved them. His parents, like himself, were noted for their humane treatment of their peasants, and for their strict abstention from all measures of arbitrary violence. I have frequently heard the more aged moujiks of Yásnaya Poliána speak of this with un-affected gratitude. Long before the issue of the manifesto of February 19, 1861, which granted freedom to every serf in Russia, and later, when he acted as Arbi-trator of the Peace, Count Tolstoy, not-withstanding his other numerous occupations, found time to busy himself with the pro-motion of the education of the poorer classes. There is no occasion to cite or

refer to his numerous essays on the subject.
As long as the family resided perpetually
on the Poliána estate, his children, from
their tenth year, were engaged, during the
winter months, in teaching the peasant
children.

In the articles I have just referred to
Count Tolstoy points out how, owing to their
idea that progress and civilisation are the
sole aim of education, the intelligent and
cultured classes of our society are incom-
petent and unfit to teach the people what
they require and wish to be taught. He
therefore proposed to form from among the
ranks of the people themselves teachers for
our national schools. For this purpose he
drew up the project of a College for
Teachers, which he wished to establish at
Yásnaya Poliána, and of which he should
have the direction and control. In carrying
his plan into execution he desired to have
the co-operation of the Yemstvo, or local
administration, and it may be said that from

first to last he met with their warmest sympathy and support. Although he had up to that time always refrained from taking part in any election, and refused to allow himself to be nominated to a public place of office, he was unanimously chosen to be a member of the council of the proposed college, and accepted the post. Unfortunately, the project failed to obtain the approval of the authorities at St. Petersburg, and the scheme fell through. It would be invidious to enter into the reasons of its rejection. I only know that the Count's sole wish and aim were to train teachers who were born in the same rank and lived the same life as the children whom they were to instruct, and that the education to be received by their scholars should not tend to create in them new desires save those of a spiritual nature, or render them unfit for the performance of the duties to which they were called by their position in life. In a letter, dated November 20, 1874, the

time when he was most actively occupied
with his new scheme, his wife wrote to me
as follows :—

"Our usual serious winter work goes on
with its accustomed regularity. Leo is
quite taken up with popular education,
schools and colleges for teachers, in which
model teachers for our national schools are
to be trained. All this keeps him busily
employed from morning till night. I cannot say that I am pleased with all this. I
regret that he should waste on such schemes
time and talent that might be far better
devoted to writing a novel. Nor do I
see that it can bring any great profit,
since all his activity is restricted to one
little corner of Russia, the Krapievinsky
district."

Of Leo Nicholaevitch's religious opinions
I know little more than what all can gather
from his works.

From what I have already said of his
youth, we may conclude that he then

accepted the creed and faith of the Orthodox Church, since he frequented her services
and went regularly to confession. As to
the years immediately preceding and following his marriage, I can state that the
confession attributed to Levine in "Anna
Karénina" is in all points identical with
the confession he himself made before his
wedding in September 1862.

I was in my seventeenth or eighteenth
year when, together with one of my
school friends, I became sorely troubled
as to the state of our souls, and, under
the influence of the teaching of the Church,
we determined to enter a monastery.
Nothing could exceed the tact and caution
with which Leo Nicholaevitch received the
announcement of my intention. Whenever
I came to him with questions, or to lay
before him my doubts, he always managed
to avoid expressing his own opinion, as if
he knew what authority he had over me,
and did not wish to bias me or, in any

way hamper my freedom. He left it to
me to work out my difficulties myself.
Once, however, he spoke out with sufficient
plainness. We were riding past the village
church wherein his parents lay buried.
Two horses were grazing in the church-
yard. We had been talking over the
only subject that then interested me.

"How can a man live in peace," I asked,
"so long as he has not solved the question
of a future life?"

"You see those two horses grazing
there," he answered; "are they not lay-
ing up for a future life?"

"But I am speaking of our spiritual,
not our earthly life."

"Indeed? Well, concerning that I neither
know nor can know anything."

Some of Leo Nicholaevitch's ancestors
and relatives, his aunt, P. I. Youschkova,
among the number, had in their old age
embraced a monastic life. His aunt, I
may add, whilst a nun, paid more than

one visit to Yásnaya Poliána, and it was there that, after a few days' illness, she died.

It was in 1876 that a change came over Leo Nicholaevitch's religious ideas and mode of life. He then began to attend punctually the services of the Church, and every morning retired to his room, in order that he might, to use his own words, commune with God. He also made a pilgrimage on foot to the famous monastery Optunine, in the government of Kalouga. He lost much of his former gaiety, and evidently strove to cultivate a gentler and humbler spirit. It was at this period, in September 1878, that I ceased to spend my summers with him. My sister wrote to me, soon after I had arrived in the Caucasus, telling me that he had become a true Gospel Christian.

There is no need to enter into details on the increasing zeal with which he surrendered himself to a religious life. He himself has told the story in his "Confession: In what consists my Faith," and "What is our Life?" Almost contemporaneously with these productions appeared his "Commentary on the Gospels," which book, as we all know, was solemnly burned in public, by order of the Synod.

If, as must be the case with men of genius, the spiritual life and faculties were wider and stronger with Leo Nicholaevitch than others, we may form a faint idea how great his sufferings were when religious doubts began to torment him, and, in his own words, all but drove him to suicide. Knowing him, as I have for so many years, I confess I read with shuddering the picture he gives in his "Confession" of his spiritual agony and sufferings. The storm these doubts raised within him, if compared with the spiritual struggles of ordinary men, was like the stir of a tempestuous sea in contrast with the rippling agitation of a small lake.

It is strange that, at the very time he

began to change his religious opinions, he not only had the monuments erected in memory of his parents, but the portraits of his ancestors and family seals repaired and cleaned. Of course the coincidence may be nothing more than accidental.

If pride and vanity be common to all men, we shall judge these traits in the character of Leo Nicholaevitch with more than ordinary indulgence.

He has in my presence acknowledged that he was both proud and vain. He loved the people, but his love for the aristocracy was still stronger. He was a born aristocrat, and had no sympathy with the middle class. When, after his youthful failures, he succeeded in winning to himself fame as a writer, he assured me that nothing had ever brought him greater happiness than his success. He acknowledged that he was pleased to think he was both writer and aristocrat. If he chanced to be told of the appointment of an old colleague or acquaintance to some important post, he always reminded me, by the remarks with which he invariably received such news, of our famous Souvaroff. He would speak of the life led in court circles, with which he was well acquainted, owing to his family connections, and affirmed that the higher places were never given for good or faithful service, but were rather conferred on those who had the good fortune and cunning to please and flatter the great. "For myself," he laughingly exclaimed, "I have never merited the rank of general in the artillery, but for all that I have won my generalship in literature." I remember once we were out shooting, when I told him that his novels, and particularly his "War and Peace," were our favourite reading at the Law School, and that we preferred his works to those of our other writers. With tears of joy in his eyes, he declared he had never had his self-love so pleasantly flattered, "since it is the young who best appreciate beauty and poetry." He then began to speak of Poushkin, and of the special features that distinguished his works from his own productions. He believed that Poushkin's best works were those written in prose. The main difference between his compositions and those of Poushkin was that, when he introduced any artistic detail, Poushkin did it with the utmost ease, and never troubled himself as to whether it would be noticed or understood by the reader. He, as it were, just put it before the reader, and then left it, never caring to expound or interpret it.

For journalists and critics he entertained a strong feeling of contempt, and was indignant with any one who dared to class them with writers, even of the lowest rank. He believed that the true mission of the press had been degraded and lost sight of in our days by the publication of much that is unnecessary, uninteresting, and, worst of all, inartistic. Criticisms of his own works he never read, nor did they seem to interest him. One of the few exceptions he made was in favour of N. Strachoff, whose judgment he highly esteemed, and with whom he has been wont to consult throughout his literary career.

In the epilogue to his novel, "Anna Karénina," he falls foul of the Russian volunteers who took part in the Servian war against Turkey. When the manuscript of the epilogue was sent to the editor of the *Russian Messenger*, the journal in which the novel originally appeared, M. Katkoff, who had been advocating in his newspaper, the *Moscow Gazette*, opinions diametrically opposed to the views of the Count, returned the manuscript with numerous corrections in the margin, accompanied by a note in which he informed the novelist that it could not be printed in his magazine unless these corrections were accepted. Leo Nicholaevitch was extremely angry at the idea that a mere journalist should dare to change a word in anything he had written, and at once dispatched a sharply written letter to the offending editor. The result was a rupture between the two, and the epilogue was issued in a separate form.

Leo Nicholaevitch never read newspapers, and considered them to be both useless and injurious, since they constantly propagate false news and erroneous ideas. He sometimes amused himself with writing essays in parody, in which the newspaper style was closely copied.

His feeling towards the periodical press in general had for its source his intense dislike to the exploitation of productions of art. A contemptuous smile was the only answer he ever deigned to make to any insinuation that the creations of an artist were produced for sale like common market wares.

There is no doubt that Levine is the portrait of the novelist himself, but this is true only to a certain extent. On this point he has explained to me that he had represented Levine to be extremely simple, in order to bring him into still greater contrast with the representatives of high life in Moscow and St. Petersburg.

Leo Nicholaevitch did not like photographs, and rarely allowed himself to be taken, and, when he did so, immediately destroyed the negative—he preferred the poorest painting to the most finished photograph.

When spiritism was beginning to come into fashion with us, he chanced to pay a visit to the late professor of chemistry, Butleroff, and was surprised to find him a firm believer in table-turning and the like phenomena. This visit, probably, inspired him with the idea of writing his comedy, "The Fruits of Enlightenment," and in "Anna Karénina" Levine is made to condemn spiritism in the exact terms employed by the Count.

The popular saying, "a nobleman without money is like a horse without oats," as he has told me, led him to take all possible means to provide for the future of his children. In the management of his estate he therefore adopted the widest and most energetic measures. He had it well stocked with thorough-bred cattle, laid out orchards, planted whole tracts of timber, and also commenced rearing bees. For the most part he himself directed everything at Yásnaya Poliána, whilst intrusting his other estates to the care of experienced stewards.

Leo Nicholaevitch's favourite amusement was shooting. All his life, till his religious opinions effected a complete change in his views and his conduct of life, he was a keen and eager sportsman. Into nearly all his novels he has introduced sporting scenes. Thus, in his " Childhood," he gives a minute and animated description of his first experience in hare-hunting, and in his " Tales for Children " he gives the full history of his two dogs, Boulka and Milton, having preserved their actual names. Besides bear-hunting, deer-stalking, and pheasant-shooting, during his stay in the Caucasus he took part in the original but high-spirited sport known under the name of strepet-shooting, the strepet being a steppe grouse. Towards the middle of August these birds, before the autumnal migration, collect in enormous flocks, and are at that time excessively wild and on the alert. Even with the utmost caution it is only possible to get within six or seven hundred feet of a flock. The Count used to ride out to the strepets on a horse expressly trained for the purpose, and after riding at foot pace two or three times round the covey, taking care each time to narrow the circle till he was at a distance of from six to seven hundred feet, dashed forth at a full gallop with loaded gun in readiness. The instant the birds rose, he dropped the reins on the neck of the horse, and the animal, understanding the signal, pulled up sharp, and thus enabled him to shoot.

His love of sport was the cause of two serious accidents. Of the first he has given an account in one of his shorter tales entitled "The Desire Stronger than Necessity." He was attacked by a huge bear, and it was only shot when he was already under the beast. He still bears a trace of the encounter in the shape of a scar on his forehead. The skin of the animal is carefully preserved at Yásnaya Poliána. After his marriage he ceased bear-hunting. He met with his second accident in the third year of his marriage. He had gone out hare-hunting, mounted on a thoroughbred English horse. He had to jump a ditch, but the horse stumbled and fell heavily with his rider into the ditch. In falling he dislocated his arm. The mishap occurred at a distance of some versts from home. For a time he dragged himself along on foot, but then fell from exhaustion and pain, though he still contrived to crawl on, till a peasant with his cart happening to pass, he was put into it and brought to the waggoner's home. The surgeon of the place set the arm so clumsily that within a month an operation had to be performed. I have been told that, though chloroform was administered, it took no less than four burly fellows to hold him down and bind him to the table.

But, after all, the dominant and noblest trait in the character of Leo Nicholaevitch is his love of truth and his desire to be truthful in all that he wrote. This he has told us in the well-known passage with which he concludes his narrative, "Sevastopol in May 1855." And we all know that the personages and incidents of his stories and novels are, with scarcely an exception, taken from real life.

Gifted by nature with rare tact and delicacy, he is extremely gentle in his bearing and conduct to others. I never remember him indulging in angry language when speaking with any of his servants; but none the less they all loved him, and seemed to fear displeasing him. Nor, with all his zeal for sport, have I ever seen him whip a dog or beat his horse.

But, lastly, I would mention his strangest peculiarity. He could not bear to wake a person from his sleep, And if, when we were on a journey or at home, this had to be done, he never failed to ask me to do it for him.

I shall conclude this chapter with a brief notice of two novels he planned, but which, owing to the impossibility of treating his subject freely, he was obliged to abandon. The first of them related to the life and times of Peter the Great, the second to the Decembrists.

In a letter I received from my sister in December 1872, she writes : " Our life just now is very, very serious. All day we are terribly busy. Leo sits in his room, surrounded by a huge pile of portraits, pictures, and books, engrossed in reading, making notes, and comparing one book with another. In the evening, when the children are gone to bed, he talks over his plans with me, and discusses the scheme of his new story. At times he is quite discouraged, falls into despair, and declares that nothing will ever come of it. At other times he is inclined to set to work in earnest, and is hopeful and interested. But up to the present I can scarcely say he has even begun."

In another letter, dated a month later, she writes as follows: "As usual we are all of us very busy. The winter is our working time, just as the summer is the busy season with our peasants. Leo is still reading up the history of the times of Peter the Great, and seems to be interested in the subject. He has already sketched the leading personages of the age, as well as the daily life of the boyars and the people, though he does not as yet know what will come of it all. But it seems to me that we shall have another prose poem like 'War and Peace,' the scene, of course, being laid in the time of Peter the Great."

In a third letter, dated February 23, 1873, she once more writes: "Leo is still busy reading and making numerous quotations, but sadly complains that inspiration fails him. Every day, however, he is more and more taken up with the study of books and memoirs, written for the most part by contemporaries of Peter."

It was in the summer of 1873 that Leo Nicholaevitch finally abandoned the subject. He declared that his estimate of the personality and public acts of Peter was diametrically at variance with the prevailing opinion, and that he could find nothing in Peter or his doings that excited his interest or sympathy. I have no positive knowledge that he ever actually commenced writing his proposed work. If he did, we may be sure that every scrap has been preserved, and is in the keeping of his wife. But I never heard anything, either from her or from himself, to justify me in supposing that he did more than jot down a few fragmentary and disconnected notes.

In preparing materials for his novel concerning the Decembrists, he was more favourably circumstanced, since he was able to avail himself, not only of all that had been published on the subject, but also of a number of family diaries and journals that were placed at his disposal. In the winter of 1877 he went to St. Petersburg, in order to go over the Petropavlovsk Fortress; but he was not allowed to visit the Alexis dungeons, though it was exactly that portion of the fortress in which he was most interested. To obtain the necessary permission he had applied to the Commandant, under whom he had served in the Crimean campaign. He was received with the utmost politeness, but at the same time was informed that, whilst any one could obtain entrance to these dungeons, only three persons in the whole empire, having once entered, could leave them, namely, the Emperor, the Commandant, and the Chief of the Gendarmes. This, among other things, he told me when he had taken his place in the carriage in which I awaited his return from the Commandant. He also related to me several stories about the means of communication invented by prisoners confined in neighbouring cells, saying that it was the Decembrists who first worked out a regular alphabet of sounds, by which, after a little practice, the signification of taps on the wall was as easily comprehended as a printed book. It was with tears in his eyes that Leo Nicholaevitch also told me how a Decembrist, during his confinement in the fortress once, bribed a sentinel to buy an apple for him. The sentinel returned with a superb basket of fruit and with the money the prisoner had given him to make the purchase. It appeared that the shop-keeper had sent

F

it as a present directly he knew it was
a Decembrist who wished to be his
customer. He further cited the case of
Lounine, a colonel in the horse-guards,
as a proof of the astonishing energy of
spirit and sarcastic contempt with which
these Decembrists endured their heavy
punishment. In a letter to his sisters,
written from the galleys, Lounine had referred satirically to the appointment of
Count Kieselieff to a high post in one
of the ministries. The letter, of course,
passed through the hands of the overseer,
and its contents were made known at
St. Petersburg. Lounine was condemned
henceforth to work in chains. The overseer of the political convicts, a full major
by rank and a German by origin, was
thus able each evening to return home
from the galleys smiling and content. And
Lounine, chained in his dark underground
cell, could also smile and despise him.

But suddenly Leo Nicholaevitch abandoned all idea of continuing the work. He affirmed that the Decembrist insurrection was the result of the teaching of the French nobles, who emigrated to Russia in large numbers after the French Revolution. Many of them were glad to serve as tutors in Russian aristocratic families. It was thus he explained the fact that most of the Decembrists were Catholics. The belief that it was therefore not a national movement, but due to foreign teaching and influence, was sufficient to prevent Leo Nicholaevitch from sympathising with it.

To judge from what my sister has told me, the composition of this romance was undertaken far more seriously and with greater persistency than was the case with the other novel. But whatever was actually written, either of the one or the other, is still carefully kept under lock and key; nor have I ever been able to get a sight of either of these manuscripts.

CHAPTER V.

MY EXCURSIONS WITH COUNT TOLSTOY AND HIS FAMILY.

FROM the time I first visited Yásnaya Poliána, Leo Nicholaevitch never made any summer a single trip without taking me with him, the one exception being when he went to Moscow, where I could be of no possible use or service to him.

But whenever he went out shooting with his dogs and gun, I always accompanied him as amateur sportsman and companion. It was the same when he went out riding, or paid a visit to his brother, who lived about thirty-five versts from Yásnaya Poliána. This he did, probably, not so much for his own sake as for mine, since he knew what pleasure it gave me to be in his society.

In the autumn of 1866, Leo Nicholaevitch went to Moscow with the intention
of visiting the field of Borodino, the
scene of the famous battle in 1812. He
arrived in Moscow alone, and put up
at our house. He then asked that I
might be allowed to accompany him. My
parents consented, and I cannot describe
my delight. I was then only eleven years
of age. We did the journey in one day
with post-horses, and took up our lodging
close to the field of battle, in the monastery
erected in memory of those who had fallen
in the fight.

For two days Leo Nicholaevitch wandered
over the spot where fifty years ago a
hundred thousand men had been slaughtered,
and where we were now confronted by a
memorial statue with its golden tablets and
inscriptions. He made the minutest investi-
gations, and drew a plan of the fight, which
was afterwards published as a frontispiece to
one of the volumes of "War and Peace."

Though he related to me several stories connected with the battle, and pointed out the places occupied by Napoleon and Koutuzoff, I confess I did not attribute much importance to them, and was far more interested in playing with a little dog that followed us from the house of the guardian of the Borodino monument. I remember that, both on the field and on our way to it, the Count hunted up the few old villagers who had witnessed or participated in the fight. We learned that the late guardian of the monument had fought in the battle, and in reward for his services had received this post. It was only a few months before our visit that the sturdy veteran had died. The old man's death was unfortunate, and, in general, the Count was far from successful in his inquiries and researches.

In the winter of 1869, immediately after the completion of his novel "War and Peace," Leo Nicholaevitch began learning

Greek, a language of which he was entirely
ignorant, and pursued his studies with such
zeal that he soon began reading the classical
writers. From my own knowledge I can
vouch that, within the short space of three
months, he had made such progress that
he was able to read Herodotus with comparative ease. That winter he resided in
Moscow, and whilst there made the acquaintance of M. Leontieff, then Professor
of Greek at the Katkoff Lyceum, whom
he consulted on certain difficulties and on
the history of Greek literature. M. Leontieff
did not seem inclined to believe in the
possibility of his having learned Greek in
so short a period, and proposed that he
should translate a passage from one of the
tragedians at sight. It happened that they
differed as to the translation of two or
three lines. But after a little discussion
the professor was obliged to admit the
correctness of the Count's version.

If "War and Peace" presents a no less

vivid picture of the epoch of the national war than Poushkin's "Captain's Daughter" gives of the age of the Pougatcheff·rising in 1773, this only proves that both these writers possess the marvellous gift of recreating the past, and of throwing themselves into the souls of bygone times and incidents. We can, therefore, easily understand that his studies in classical literature carried Leo Nicholaevitch back to ages too remote and too alien from our own, and called forth in him a feeling of melancholy and despair seemingly inexplicable, but none the less strong.

His wife, alarmed at the effect they produced on him, advised him to undertake some new literary work to free himself from these impressions.

His interest in the classics gradually weakened, but his melancholy and apathy had considerably undermined his health. To restore his strength and bring back his former energy it was decided that he should drink koumis.

The Count's father had travelled to the steppes of Bashkeria to undergo a cure by drinking koumis, and he himself had been there a short time before his marriage.

In the beginning of the summer of 1870 we arrived in the Nicholaieff district of the government of Samara, and thence struck off eastward, and, following along the banks of the Karalieck, finally reached the village bearing the name of the river.

Leo Nicholaevitch never travelled by second class; and during this journey we went third class, first by rail as far as Nijhni Novgorod, and then by the Volga steamboat to Samara, from which point we had a hundred and twenty versts to make on horseback.

On the steamboat he was greatly interested in observing the habits and learning the life of the pastoral tribes peopling the flats of the Lower Volga.

Leo Nicholaevitch possesses a remarkable talent for making himself agreeable to strange passengers; and if, by chance, he falls into the company of reserved or surly persons, after a few attempts he is always sure to succeed in winning them over and inducing them to chat freely and at their ease. He knows exactly how to gain their confidence, and himself takes an unaffected interest in all they may relate of themselves and their affairs. And so it was now. Before the second day was over he had got to be on the friendliest terms with all on deck, not excepting the simple-minded sailors, with whom we passed the whole night in the fore-part of the vessel.

In Karalieck he was welcomed as an old acquaintance. We put up in a tent belonging to a mullah, who together with his family lived in an adjoining tent.

It is not every one who has had the chance to see one of these tents, or *Kot-chévka*, as it is called. It is like a wooden cage of a longish hemispherical shape. This cage is covered with thick felt, and

is provided with a tiny painted door. Soft
feather grass serves as a carpet. The tent
admits of being easily taken to pieces and
transported from place to place. It is
admirably suited for a summer residence
in the steppes.

Whilst undergoing the koumis treatment,
it is well to follow strictly the example of
the Bashkirs, and to refrain from all meal
and vegetable food, and restrict oneself to
meat. Leo Nicholaevitch was very particular
in observing the required diet, and consequently derived no little good from the
treatment.

Besides ourselves, there were other
koumis drinkers at Karalieck, but they
had put themselves, as it were, in quaran-
tine, and refused to associate with, or in
any way to adopt the life of, Bashkir
nomads.

But very soon after his arrival Leo
Nicholaevitch struck up acquaintance with
them, and, thanks to his genial influence,

the place grew gay and lively. A teacher
at one of our seminaries, in spite of his
age, tried skipping-rope matches with him;
an attorney's chief clerk liked to debate
with him on questions of literature and
philosophy; and a young farmer from the
government of Samara became one of his
devoted and attached followers.

We made up a party of four, and set
out for a long drive through the Bashkir
villages. We took our guns, and furnished
ourselves with numerous presents. On our
way we had some first-rate duck shooting,
and generally passed our nights in a
kotchévka, where we were regaled with
koumis. If, by chance, Leo Nicholaevitch
admired any particular animal in a herd
of horses let loose on the steppe, or said
to me, "Look, what a splendid mare for
giving milk," when we took leave of the
good people an hour or so later, our
host would be seen putting the same
horse to our *tarantass*, and would force

us to accept it as a present. Of course
when we passed the tent on our way
back, we took care to make some suitable
present in return.

The Count found the simple easy life
of these Bashkirs to be full of real poetry.
He was well acquainted with their habits
and customs; they had long known him,
and learned to love him, and always spoke
of him as "the Count," there being no
other Count for them. Among them all,
a certain Chadziemourat, whom we Russians
knew as Michael Ivanoff, was perhaps most
attached to him. He was fond of a joke,
was very nimble and active in his move-
ments, was full of dry humour, and was a
good player at draughts.

Our visit to the steppes extended altogether over six weeks, during which time
the Count and myself went to the Petrov-
sky fair held at Bozoulouk, a small town
about seventy versts distant. The fair
attracted a strange motley of different

nationalities and races, Russian moujiks, Ural Cossacks, Bashkirs, and Khirgese. As usual, and thanks to his natural affability, Leo Nicholaevitch was soon on the best terms with them all. Some of the frequenters of the fair were generally drunk, but, for all that, the Count would chat and laugh with them. Once a drunken moujik, inspired by a superfluous excess of affection, wished to embrace him, but a stern look from the Count was sufficient to make him draw back, as he muttered a kind of apology, " No, pardon me, I pray you."

During our wanderings on the steppes, Leo Nicholaevitch was, perhaps, most interested in mixing with members of the Molochan sect, and particularly their venerable chief and teacher, Aglaia. Together with some of the clergy of the place, he more than once had discussions with these dissidents, his object being not so much to convince them as to learn authoritatively the points on which they differed from the Orthodox Church. They acknowledge no guide save the Scriptures, reject all tradition, and observe none of the ordinary rites and ceremonies of the Church. They have no places set apart for public worship, pay no reverence to images, and have no priests or clergy of any kind. By fasting they understand abstinence in general, and not merely refraining from certain articles of food. For this reason, they do not keep from milk when fasting, and, as some have supposed, they are therefore called Molochanic, or Milk Drinkers. It is worthy of note that these sectarians are distinguished by an honesty and a love of work which we do not remark among their Orthodox neighbours. They further abstain from all intoxicating drinks. Their recruits are almost exclusively made from the peasant and uncultured classes.

I was very pleased when I was allowed, without a word from Leo Nicholaevitch, to make use of a huge Greek lexicon he had brought with him for pressing between its leaves a considerable collection of flowers peculiar to the steppe districts of Samara. It showed that his classical studies had lost the absorbing interest they once possessed for him.

On our return home, evidently under the influence of what he had seen and heard among the Bashkirs, Leo Nicholaevitch read through the Koran in a French translation.

Whilst drinking koumis, he had looked over an estate of two thousand acres that was for sale, and in the following winter purchased it. A peasant was sent out from Yásnaya Poliána to undertake its management and to build a farmhouse. Two years later, we all spent the summer on his new estate.

A Bashkir from Karalieck, famous for its herds of mares, was engaged for the Yásnaya Poliána estate, and he soon arrived in a small *teleiga*, together with his wife and a removable tent.

Mahometschach, or as he was called in Russian Romanovitch, was steady, civil, and precise in character, and it was for these qualities that he had been chosen. The interior of the tent was kept cleanly and even luxuriously, and we often went to see him, not to drink koumis, but to sit and chat with him. In the centre of the tent a carpet was laid down with some cushions, whilst at one of the sides was placed a table with two chairs. These latter accessories were intended expressly for us. On one of the walls a highly ornamented saddle was hung up. One side of the tent was curtained with bright chintz hangings, behind which his wife retired whenever any male visitor appeared. From behind them she used to hand her husband bottles of koumis and glasses on a wooden platter. Leo Nicholaevitch jokingly named the kotchévka our saloon.

G

Romanovitch was very proud of our visits, the more so as it was the only distraction he had, since, like most well-to-do Bashkirs, he never amused or interested himself with any kind of occupation.

It was in the same year that for the first time the whole estate was ploughed and sown. Unfortunately the crops failed everywhere, and a famine, known as the Samara famine, ensued. It is impossible to give an adequate idea of the misery and sufferings the poorer peasants had to endure. With his wonted kindliness and energy, Leo Nicholaevitch came to their aid, and was the first to open a subscription fund for the starving population. I accompanied him to two of the neighbouring villages, and helped him to make an inventory of all the grain and property actually in their possession. For this purpose we selected every third village. Nothing could be more piteous than the eagerness with which the peasants prayed us to insert their names in

the inventory, imagining that only those
whose property was catalogued would receive any help. Leo Nicholaevitch wrote
an article in which he drew a truthful picture of the famine-stricken districts. The
article was sent to the editor of the *Moscow
News*, together with a hundred roubles as
a first subscription for the initiation of the
good work.

In 1878 we spent a second summer on
the Samara estate. An adjoining estate
of four thousand acres had been bought
by the Count during the preceding winter.
Romanovitch, with his mares and the
" saloon," was again engaged. Besides his
own tent, another was put up especially for
our use and accommodation. In the course
of the summer Leo Nicholaevitch arranged
a sporting festival that was quite a novelty
in these places. Romanovitch was autho-
rised to announce to the peasants and neighbours that races were to be run on the
Count's estate, the principal one being fifty

versts' distance. The neighbouring Bashkirs, Ural Cossacks, and Russian moujiks
all alike took interest in the coming races.
The prizes were an ox, a horse, a gun, a
clock, a dressing-gown, and other articles,
and invitations were sent out to all who
were likely to take part in the sport. We
ourselves levelled and cleared the course,
measured off a large circle five versts in
length, and erected the starting-post. For
the dinner that was to follow huge joints
of mutton and horse-flesh, and other dainties
were provided. On the appointed day
a crowd of several thousand people was
collected. The Bashkirs and Khirgese arrived with their tents, plenty of koumis,
boiling - coppers, and sheep. The wild
steppe covered with high grass, the long
line of tents arranged on either side, and
the motley crowd of eager lively spectators,
combined to make a varied and interesting
picture. The summits of the hillocks, called
shieschkie, were spread with carpets and felt

mats, on which the wealthier Bashkirs were to be seen squatting, with their legs tucked under them. In the centre of the group a young Bashkir was busy pouring out and handing round to each in turn a cup of koumis. From different points in the crowd could be heard snatches of song to the accompaniment of reed-pipes, chanted in a drawling tone that struck the European ear somewhat sadly. Here and there were to be seen wrestlers showing off their skill and practice in an art in which the Bashkirs particularly excel. As I watched the scene my mind went back to the long-distant days when Russia lay under the Tartar yoke. The runners for the chief race brought with them thirty trained horses. The riders were boys of about ten years, and they rode without saddles. The race lasted exactly an hour and forty minutes. Consequently it was run at the rate of two minutes a verst. Of the thirty horses, ten ran the whole distance, the others giving up. The festival lasted two days, and passed off very gaily, and in the most perfect order. What, probably, pleased the Count most was the complete absence of the police. All the guests seemed to be heartily contented with the amusements provided for them, and more than once expressed their full gratitude to their host.

This was destined to be the last of my summer vacations at Yásnaya Poliána, for I now entered on my new service. When I told Leo Nicholaevitch that I was going to serve in the Caucasus, he exclaimed, "You are too late for the Caucasus. The whole country now stinks of tchinovniks!"

The thought of a long separation from those I loved so warmly, and the necessity of soon bidding farewell to a family in whose circle I had spent the happiest years of my life, made me quite ill, and for some days I was obliged to keep my bed. The innocent cause of my malady instinctively guessed its real origin, and did all that lay in his power to cheer and console me. For hours he would sit with me, and advise me not to be too exacting when I found myself in a strange country, but to accommodate myself, as far as possible, to its mode of life, and to take interest in all that concerned the people with whom I was about to make my home. The better to fit me for my new surroundings, he read to me some chapters of his manuscript reminiscences of the Caucasus.

On the eleventh of September 1878, I said good-bye to them, and set off for my new post, All who have so far read my reminiscences of the Count will share my respect and esteem for the man, and for the life he has led. Nor must it be supposed that I have purposely suppressed anything that might not tell to his advantage. Such a supposition would be entirely erroneous. I am, at least, aware of nothing in his life that needs to be concealed from the knowledge of the reader.

There is no doubt that all this time the intellectual and moral life of the Count was slowly tending in many respects to his life of the actual moment.

His kindly relations with the peasant classes, his denial of the benefits of civilisation, his simplicity in the arrangement and surroundings of his home, the exemplariness of his family life, his wide and enlightened views on education, his devotion to truth and work, his desire to attain, as far as possible, perfection (to which desire he remained faithful all his life), his considerateness and respect, coupled with a disinterested and unselfish love for his neighbour, and lastly, his denial of the right to exercise force or violence in our dealings with our fellow-creatures—all these qualities of his moral and intellectual character form the ground and basis of his later teaching, and free it entirely of anything that smacks of eccentricity or affectedness.

CHAPTER VI.

NINE years had passed. I had gradually
become accustomed to my new sphere of
activity. It was only at rare intervals that
I had received any news from Yásnaya
Poliána, where all this time Leo Nicholaevitch was earnestly striving to work out
the common problem of humanity.

After my long sojourn in the extreme
frontier districts of European Russia, I
had, in 1887, the pleasure of once more
visiting Moscow, my native city, and in
the beginning of August was already in
Yásnaya Poliána.

I arrived at the time when Leo Nicholaevitch was writing the concluding chapters of his "Kreutzer Sonata," that is, when he had already completed his ethical system.

My sister, with all the pride natural to a mother, watched her children as they noisily rushed out to meet me, and laughingly asked me, "Do you recognise her?" or exclaimed, "Look, she is taller than you now!" But Leo Nicholaevitch did not as yet make his appearance, and I began to ask after him. A few minutes later his study door opened, and he came into the ante-room to welcome me. His greeting was friendly, but there was a seriousness in his tone which made me feel that my joy at being again in his company would no longer be of the kind it was in former days.

Although during these nine years he had considerably aged, and his hair had grown greyer, the change was by no means so marked as might have been expected. But at the same time his face wore marks of

the severe spiritual struggle he had undergone.   I was most struck by the quiet
but sad expression his features bore.   I remembered his look of earlier years.   Now
his face produced cn me the same impression I experienced when I first read his
"Confession."

I spent nearly two months at Yásnaya
Poliána, and whilst there, made myself
acquainted with the creed taught by Leo
Nicholaevitch, and had numerous oppor-
tunities of seeing how his relations regarded
his teaching, and how both he and his
family now lived.

All this it will be my object to relate
in this, the last chapter of my reminiscences.

As might be supposed, his teaching was
diversely received by the public at large.

I have been told that he received letters
from all quarters of the world, some written
by his followers, others by his opponents.
I can imagine his disciples wishing to ex-

change ideas with their teacher, but, I confess, I do not understand why his opponents
troubled him with their letters. In many
cases, persons who have never read a line of
his works wrote simply to vent their disapproval of doctrines erroneously attributed
to him. Such correspondents, he has told
me, he regarded with pity, though he felt
sure that their opposition to his creed was
due entirely to their ignorance of what he
really taught. "The more men read my
books," he said, "the less inclined they will
be to reject my teaching."

To my surprise, I have never yet met
with a true and accurate exposition of his
creed; even the so-called Tolstoists do not
seem to have thoroughly grasped its real
meaning.

The foundation of his creed is the Gospel
law of love to our neighbours. On this
law his entire system is constructed, and
is summed up in three general rules or
principles.

These three rules are set forth by Leo Nicholaevitch as necessary to the welfare and development of mankind, and any departure from them must involve the decadence of the individual, and bring with it pain and suffering.

They are the following : That we should not oppose evil with force ; That we should not consume more than we ourselves produce ; That men and women should equally practise and aspire towards purity and chastity.

Without entering into a close analysis or estimate of his teaching, which does not come within the province of my task, I shall only discuss these principles so far as Leo Nicholaevitch himself explained them to me.

The chief and most serious objection to the first rule is based on the proposition that human life is a struggle for existence, a struggle that has to be carried on not only with nature, but with our fellow-creatures.

This struggle between man and man is not only a condition, but a governing factor in the development of humanity, that is, of progress ; and, therefore, the rule laid down, even if theoretically sound, cannot be put into practice.

In reply to this objection, Leo Nicholae-vitch proposed that each man should seriously put to himself the question whether love or antagonism to our neighbour be a quality inherent in human nature. And, admitting that we may find this truth hard to under-stand, we should further ask ourselves how is it that, if a kindly relation to our neigh-bour, to our children, to our servants, and even to our animals is more profitable and also more pleasant to ourselves, force and violence should be necessary in our relation to all other men.

If the principle of love to our neighbour be a self-proved truth, it is in vain that men have created for themselves the law of a struggle for existence with their neighbour, when they cannot escape the struggle with nature for that existence.

This, from his point of view, immoral law of the right to practise violence, first of all diverts men from the necessary struggle with nature, and weakens their strength for such struggle; and, secondly, it increases crime, contributes to divide men and to oppose race to race, and in general conduces to our moral and physical degradation, whilst it can in no way aid the progressive development of humanity.

With each year Leo Nicholaevitch has become more decided and more vehement in his hostility to progress, in the sense in which that term is understood by his contemporaries.

In his opinion, modern progress, availing itself of economical theories, creates money distractions and makes money the criterion of worth and position. But by means of money a man can reduce his neighbour to a state of lower degradation than any to which mere ordinary slavery can ever bring him; for by aid of the almighty rouble this lower form of enslavement is effected in an underhand way and with impunity, and consequently without pity or remorse.

Further, this progress creates a necessity for railways and easy ways of communication, together with rivalry and concurrence in commerce and trade, and thus inevitably leads to the rapid and unequal distribution of wealth among men.

Once such a state of things exists, it is wrong in us quietly to accept it, or to allow its continuance, whilst all the time we theoretically admit it is an evil, and the outcome of an immoral struggle for superiority over our neighbour. We should rather seek some escape from it, and the more so because such escape is within our grasp and easy to be found.

"The time will come," he said to me, "when men will be convinced of the truthfulness of my teaching. And then,

without doubt, they will adopt a different
and a better formula of progress. Then
the struggle with nature, now so burden-
some, will be made lighter, and we shall
be able to attain a higher and more general
state of happiness."

Objections to the second rule are generally based on the supposed fact that men
naturally seek to gain the most they can for
themselves.

If the observance of the first rule must
bring with it a practical gain, Leo Nicholaevitch does not have recourse to any like
argument in his refutation of this objection
to the second rule, but contents himself
with simply declaring that an act of volun-
tary self-denial in favour of our neighbour
is always easier than those compulsory acts
of self-denial which the majority of men have
to make.

But it must not be supposed that Leo
Nicholaevitch bases his teaching on personal
and self-interested considerations of this kind.

They are only used to show that the arguments commonly advanced against his teaching may be reasonably urged in its favour. His creed is founded on the great moral truth of love to our neighbour, which does not require to be proved, since it is natural to and inherent in us all.

This truth, in his opinion, still lives and has not lost its force, but, in opposition to economical progress, must daily gain in strength. He has insisted on this idea in his later productions, where he declares that men live only by love.

The third rule that men and women should equally practise and aspire towards purity and chastity forms the theme of his novel the " Kreutzer Sonata."

Although, by way of answer to the questions put to him by numerous critics and correspondents as to the view this novel is designed to advocate, the Count has appended to its later editions a "post-preface," as he terms it, in which he explains the object with which he wrote his work, still most of his readers seem to have failed to discover in it the first real solution of the so-called woman's question. On the contrary, they all cry out that it preaches asceticism, and upholds a monastic life as our ideal. Such an interpretation can only proceed from an unwillingness or an inability to understand his views on the conception of morality current among the men of our days.

In the "Kreutzer Sonata" he maintains that modern society allows a man before his marriage, and even after his marriage, when his wife grows a little old, to take other women, but at the same time requires the wife to continue to be pure and chaste.

By thus demanding more of the woman than of the man, we degrade women, and they are made to be nothing more than the slaves of men's physical desires.

The degrading enslavement of women in contemporary society is shown in this, that

the purest of girls are, as it were, exhibited
at our balls for sale to young men who, if
they have not already worn away their
health in vice and become thoroughly
corrupt, have at least no pretence to be
pure. And such a man is considered to
be conferring a great honour on any girl
he may choose to ask to be his wife.
And to tempt him to do this, she is
paraded for sale in an indecently low-cut
costume, whilst he is further enticed on
by having his vanity humoured in being
privileged to take the initiatory step in
choosing a wife. At the same time, that
too severe demands may not be made
upon him, houses of vice are tolerated
and allowed to exist for his pleasure and
amusement.

The complete enslavement of women is
also proved by the fact that nine-tenths of
our shops deal almost exclusively in articles
designed for the dressing up and adornment
of women.

From this inequality, and from this degradation of our women, we reap the natural result, and need not be astonished if so few marriages bring happiness.

This idea underlies the picture he gives of the seemingly gratuitous quarrels and misunderstandings that are constantly arising between Posdniescheff and his wife. In reality they are caused by nothing else than the degradation of the woman and the consequent inequality in the relations between husband and wife.

In the "Kreutzer Sonata" the novelist exposes the faulty organisation of contemporary family life, and attributes its abnormal defects to the same cause, the degrading position occupied by women.

When some thirty years ago, under the influence of the liberal ideas then in vogue, this question as to woman's true position was first prominently brought forward, it was solved, as Leo Nicholaevitch thinks, not with the object of putting the woman on a level and equal rank with the man. Her equality was supposed to be secured by giving her the right to vote at elections, to exercise the profession of doctor, to serve in public offices — in a word, by granting her full power to alienate herself from all home duties, and to enjoy the same liberty of vice as men have long ago claimed for themselves. In this way her equality with man, to use the Count's own words, consists solely in that, inasmuch as men are free to lead depraved lives, henceforth the same freedom shall be extended to women.

In the opening pages of his " Kreutzer Sonata" the novelist has put these opinions into the mouth of the lawyer and the lady passenger in the railway carriage; and in the same scene we have the merchant with his old-fashioned ideas on the woman's question, in accordance with which he claims full liberty to amuse himself, whenever the fancy seizes him, with fallen beauties, all the while naturally expecting his wife to remain faithful and to observe the strict moral law. We cannot read this chapter without perceiving that, in the opinion of the novelist, the merchant is nearer to the truth than either the lawyer or the lady traveller.

And thus, a full and real equality between man and woman can only be secured—not by the degradation of the woman, but by the elevation of the man. The novel, therefore, teaches that men, no less than women, should lead pure lives before marriage, and afterwards remain true and faithful to one wife.

To prove the soundness of this principle, the ideal held up for our achievement is like purity and like chastity in all. And in evidence of the justice of this view, we are reminded of the feeling of shame we all experience when for the first time we have erred and lost our innocence.

In his opinion, as set forth in the same
novel, it is not sufficient for us to preserve
our purity before marriage, and after
marriage to remain faithful to one wife.
To fulfil the higher law of our being, and
to attain the ideal set before us, we must
discourage all that, as society is now constituted, is born of the rivalry and struggle
created by the actual inequality of the
sexes.   For this reason we must abandon
the custom of dressing up women solely
with the aim of attracting men.   By means
of a healthier education we must eradicate
the coquetry that has now become an in-
tuitive quality in women.   In a word, in
all our social relations, we must discourage
everything that is calculated to excite
sexual passions or to awaken impure
desires.   Only then can we hope for a
true and perfect equality between man and
woman.   Only then will the inequality
that reigns now disappear of itself, even
in the sphere of abstract activity.

It is on this ground that many of his critics have accused Leo Nicholaevitch of teaching asceticism.

I shall now proceed to touch on the change his creed has effected in the character and life of Count Tolstoy.

Only a genial nature could submit to a change so complete as that undergone by Leo Nicholaevitch in obedience to the creed he has finally accepted. The change that has taken place in his entire personality within these last ten years is in the true sense of the word a full and radical change. Not only has his life and his every relation to men and creatures changed, but we remark a similar change in his sphere and mode of thought. And if he still remains faithful to some of his earlier views, such as his antagonism to progress and civilisation, these views have no longer the same basis and foundation.

The whole individuality of the man has been transformed into a personification of the idea of love to his neighbour. And, if I may be pardoned the paradox, I should say that his error consists in thinking it to be a departure from his views, though he does it for the sake of the idea itself, when he sharply condemns another for his ill deeds.

As love to his neighbour is the fundamental axiom of his creed, in the same way this idea now serves as the basis of each of his separate and distinct convictions.

I do not wish to dwell on some of his present opinions, and to point out how he adapts them to life in general and to his own surroundings in particular.

Literature and art, whilst continuing to be the interpreters of beauty and poetry, must in their works also remain true to this idea of love. All his later productions have, therefore this exclusive characteristic. He now looks on all his earlier compositions as being hurtful, because in them he describes and portrays love only in its lower and ordinary aspects.

His educational theories as to liberty in the choice of subjects being allowed to the pupil, and the complete absence of all compulsory measures on the part of the teacher, were formerly insisted on for the sake of promoting culture and enlightenment, but are now advocated by him solely in accordance with his denial of the right to employ force or violence. Instruction and the knowledge of nature, of man, and of life are beneficial only so far as they contribute to the good of our neighbours; but, as manifestations of progress and the cause of the enslavement of our neighbour, they are on the contrary prejudicial and hurtful. This evil he finds to be the leading trait in our modern system of education, since the only aim it has in view is to secure for the learner a higher position in society than that occupied by his neighbour, to enable him to show his superiority, and to afford him the means of forcing his neighbour to serve and submit to him. He consequently believed it to be his duty to cease busying himself with the education of his children, and was displeased when his wife continued to do so. When his eldest son, having just finished his university studies, consulted him as to what career in life he should adopt, his father advised him to go and be a fellow-worker with the moujik.

The aim of education should be to awaken and develop sympathy and love for our neighbour, and, in opposition to what is generally done in modern society, to dull, rather than foster, the sensual passions. At the same time, education should cultivate a love of simplicity and an aversion to luxury. True and well-timed courtesy proves love to our neighbours, but courtesy as too often practised in our days, with its officious affectation, is to be condemned, since it is but the outcome of calculating egotism. Inasmuch as the moral culture and instruction of his children had always been conducted in accordance with these principles, we cannot say that any change has come over his views on education, unless we take into account the fact that Leo Nicholaevitch himself likes to employ the language and style of the people in testimony of that simplicity, the observance of which he recommends in every act of our lives.

Formerly he regarded civilisation as hurtful, because it weakens and effeminates men, thus rendering them unfit for the struggle they have to wage with nature; but now he finds it to be chiefly prejudicial in that it necessarily involves the exploitation of our neighbour's labour, without which it is impossible for us to possess comforts and luxuries. He goes so far as to condemn not only comfort and luxury, but even cleanliness, if it is to be procured by the services and labour of others. How this principle is applied to his own home-life we shall see a little later on; for the moment it is enough to say that he always himself heats his bath and fetches the water for it. The water with which his washing-stand is daily supplied is also fetched by himself.

It is on the same ground that he denies the utility of railroads, and always does his best to avoid making use of them.

The former estimate of the aristocracy is now replaced by pity for the peasantry. The lower a man stands in the social scale, the more keenly he should call forth our love and pity. In this respect, it is worthy of note that, in his drama, "The Power of Darkness," the brightest of the personages is Achime with his theories on money and banks. The love he feels for the people, and the interest he takes in their well-being, have, if possible, become less restricted and wider than before. For in

their mode of life, and in their conduct
towards their neighbour, they approach
nearest to his rule and standard.   Instead
of shutting himself up from the world, as
he was once inclined to do, he is now ac-
cessible to all, and is freely visited by
persons of every kind and description.   As
for the peasants, his house is always open
to them, and they come constantly, either
to consult him or to seek his help.   He
believes that we do wrong to isolate ourselves, since such a habit can only spring
from an unwillingness to see or to know
anything of the necessities and sufferings
of others.

He further teaches that property is an
evil, so long as it has to be kept and
protected by force and authority.   Concerning his own property, he told me that
he had wished to free himself from it, as
from a thing that was evil in itself, and
shackled him in living up to his convictions.   But he confessed he had acted

wrongly in seeking to burden another with the evil, that is, in trying to dispose of it. By such means he only created another evil, which took the form of a vehement protest and serious disapproval on the part of his wife. In consequence of this, he proposed to make over to her the whole property in her name; and, when she refused, he made a second equally unsuccessful proposal in favour of the children. True to his rule never to resist evil by force, and unwilling to charge another with the burden of the evil, he began to live as if he had no estate or property, refused to receive any income himself from it, or to profit by it in any way, with the sole exception of continuing to live under the roof of his house at Yásnaya Poliána. He refused all pecuniary help, on the principle that every money transaction is but the means of effecting the enslavement of our neighbour, but found it difficult to put his theory into practice, inasmuch as his family

continued to enjoy the profits of his property. My sister has told me that they
never distributed less than from three to
four thousand roubles yearly among the
poor. And I remember how once a poor,
old, decrepit moujik came and asked him
to give him some timber with which he
could repair his tumble-down sheds. The
Count invited me to go with him into the
forest, and we two, having taken our axes
with us, cut down some trees, lopped off
the branches, and piled the logs in order
on the peasant's cart. I must confess I
worked with a hearty good-will, and experienced a pleasure in the work I had
never known before. This may have been
because I was so completely under the
influence of my brother-in-law, or simply
because I was working for a sick broken-
down fellow-creature. All the time we
worked, the poor peasant's face wore an expression of quiet gratitude. Leo Nicholaevitch, noting my frame of mind, purposely

I

rewarded my zeal by allotting to me the
harder share of the work. And when we
had finished and sent the moujik away re-
joicing, he turned to me and said, " Is
it possible to doubt the necessity of helping our neighbour in distress, or the joy
which such help brings with it ? "

Although accustomed from his youth to
smoke and to drink wine, he has now
abandoned both habits, and, as is well
known, has founded temperance leagues
in the villages neighbouring his estates.

The service of dependants he neither
requires nor permits, and seldom accepts
any from those of his household, who
would thereby wish to show rather their
attachment to him than any subordination
to the head of the family. At dinner, if
a servant hands a dish to him, he is evidently displeased, though he carefully ab-
stains from refusing the proffered service,
and once more acts on his principle of
never enforcing his opinions on others, or

offending persons by making himself peculiar and different to them. As I have already remarked, he himself each day cleans up and arranges his study.

From a feeling of pity for animals, he has long abandoned hunting and shooting, and has assured me that, not only has sport lost all attraction for him, but he is now unable to understand how it could ever have afforded him pleasure. From the same motive he has become a strict vegetarian, and ceased to ride on horseback.

As an example of how he carries out his belief that we have no right to avail ourselves of the services of men or animals, I may remark that, whenever his family removes from Yásnaya Poliána, to take up their winter-quarters in Moscow, he himself does the journey on foot, though it is a distance of no less than a hundred and ninety-five versts. He has assured me that he accomplishes this distance without excessive exertion or fatigue. On such

occasions he always remains at Yásnaya
Poliána a few days longer than the rest
of the family, and, when once they are
gone, he becomes entirely his own cook
and servant. He delays his departure in
this way, lest his wife should be made
anxious about him, or know that he does
the journey on foot. Consequently, his
love for active exercise has remained un-
changed, except that he now indulges in
it for some useful end, such as plough-
ing a field, cutting down timber, or build-
ing a hut for some peasant.

His earlier aversion to doctors and medicinal treatment has of late grown intenser
and more confirmed. Two years before
my last visit Leo Nicholaevitch accidentally
hurt his foot. The pain became so intense
as to make him for a while delirious. His
wife then determined to take upon herself
the responsibility of sending for a surgeon.
The latter was received by his patient with
scant affability, and was roughly told, pro-

bably in the hope of getting rid of him, that he would not have come unless he had hoped to get a good fee. To this the surgeon quietly replied, that he wondered the very man who preached love to his neighbour should himself so flagrantly violate the rule of love. In the end, the surgeon was allowed to apply his treatment, and before long the inflammation diminished, and the refractory patient was restored to health. But the Count remained unshaken in his belief; and I remember that, during my last visit, when he was suffering, I advised him to drink Carlsbad waters, whereupon he declared, that no one had ever proved these waters to be of any use either for his illness or any other. Nor could he be persuaded to follow a regular cure.

His former gaiety of temper, which enlivened all who were near him, has now entirely disappeared. There is nothing morose or unduly sad in his present tem-

perament, but at the same time there is
no longer any trace of the boyish merriment
that was once so attractive in him. This
earlier trait in his character has, if I may
so express myself, fallen to pieces, and is
now shared by his children. Unconstrained
by his presence, they freely indulge in their
romps and mirth, and this always seemed
to me to harmonise with his concentrated
seriousness, and to give a brighter colouring to his stern views on social morality.
Though he takes no active part in their
chat, or when they sing or play at the
piano, he always seems to be interested
and pleased in what they do. On the day
of my arrival he appeared to make an
effort to throw off his seriousness, perhaps
having remarked the impression his changed
manner had produced on me, and I recollect that, as I was walking up and down
the room, he suddenly leaped up from his
chair, and with a laugh, jumping on my
back, made me carry him round two or

three times. He still retains his love for
the society of children, but does not lay
himself out to amuse them, as he used to
do. His younger sons and nephews are very
fond of playing draughts with him. But in
all this there is something mechanical : he
listens to the conversation going on around
him, but does not, after his old fashion,
take part in it, particularly if it in any
wise touches the doctrines of his creed,
and preserves an all but absolute silence.
If he talks, it is invariably on some subject
of importance, something that has to be
done, and the subject is treated by him with
gravity and seriousness.

He advised me to quit the Government
service, and change my mode of life, and he
spoke to me of the joy which the practice
of the great law, love to our neighbour,
brings with it. Amongst others, he held
up to me as an example, young Prince Hielkoff. The prince was long unacquainted
with Leo Nicholaevitch and his teaching.

Almost at the same time as his teaching was first made generally public, young Hielkoff cut all his former ties, threw up his rank as officer in the guards, and gave over his estates to his peasants, leaving for himself only ten acres of land, but, previously to taking up his residence on his little property, went to work with and amongst the moujiks. He zealously occupied himself with the commonest work, and awaited with eagerness the time when he should so far have improved that his nearest neighbour, a Jew, would be glad to engage him to come and work in his fields for five roubles a month. Only then would he allow himself to marry, probably choosing a peasant girl for his wife, and to settle with her on his ten acre estate. His adoption of the new creed, as was to be expected, brought upon him the ridicule of most of his friends, and the bitterest reproaches of his mother. I remember meeting him in the Caucasus while he was serving in the army. Notwithstanding the slightness of our acquaintance, he left a most favourable impression on me, and appeared to be a kindly hearted man.

Leo Nicholaevitch complained to me that women had especially hindered the spread and application of his teaching, and attributed this to the incapacity of women to make or accept accurate and precise definitions. When speaking once to him of the traits peculiar to women, I told him of one I had particularly remarked. The peculiarity I referred to consists in this, that a woman, when picking up anything from the ground, never bends her back, but first squats or makes a kind of courtesy and then stoops down. A man, on the contrary, will most scrupulously bend his back. I proved my assertion by getting all the women of the house to go through the experiment, and it succeeded most brilliantly, even in the case of the old nurse and the three-year-old daughter of the Count. He laughed heartily and loudly, whilst the experiment was on foot, and each of them, not knowing why we wished them to do it, picked up my little pocket-brush from the ground. We were all pleased to hear him once more laugh so freely.

But, in spite of all the change that had come over him, he continued to enjoy the love and devotion of his whole family. Their love was coupled with the deepest respect for his genius. He is now a grandfather; and, adopting his favourite way of employing the speech of the people, they like to call him "ours" or "our old man."

Nor is this reverence restricted to the family alone, for, though at his own request his name has been struck off the list of assessors of the peace, since he believes it to be wrong to take an oath or to judge a fellow-creature, he has often, as a mark of esteem, been chosen to the post of justice of the peace.

It now only remains to me to say a few words as to how his family look on and regard his teaching.

It has often been asserted in print that his family do not share his opinions and views. This would not in any case be surprising, considering that among them are his wife and four grown-up sons and daughters, each of whom most naturally has his or her peculiar convictions; but in fact such an idea is entirely erroneous.

In accordance with his rule not to oppose error by force, Leo Nicholaevitch has always endeavoured to give his children the fullest liberty to accept or reject his teaching. He has taught them what he believes to be the truth, but neither in his tone nor in his manner does he seek to impose upon them his ideas. He sets forth his doctrines, leaving it to his hearers to exercise their free judgment, but is none the less convinced himself that they must prove a blessing to those who adopt them,

assured that sooner or later they will be
generally acknowledged and accepted. He
can, therefore, only regret than men still
cling to error and forget that, unless they
be ruled by the law of love, there is and
can be no life in them. And in exactly a
similar way he regards his children. He
has told me that an insincere, or a sincere
but inoculated, adoption . of his doctrines
on the part of his children is a thing he
has always feared. His children understand this, and therefore preserve to themselves as their right the full and impartial
liberty of thought and belief.

With reference to his wife, however, I
have noticed that he is inclined to be
more exacting, and seems to be displeased
and hurt that she persists in opposing his
wish to abandon his worldly possessions,
and continues to educate her children after
the old fashion and spirit.

In her turn his wife believes that she
is right in so acting, and is grieved at

the hard necessity of having to thwart his
dearest wish.

She has been the secret witness of all
his spiritual struggle, and has with anxiety
watched the gradual development into full
growth of his religious and social creeds.
No wonder if, at times, they have filled her
with a feeling of disquietude, and she
has feared their baleful influence on the
health and well-being of her husband. This
feeling, in spite of herself, for a while
generated an aversion to his creed, and
a dread of its results. Conscious of her
powerlessness to change the current of his
thoughts, and thus render easier to him
the process of his spiritual conflict, she
felt that she could come to the aid of
her children, and therefore opposed her
husband's demands in all that threatened
their impoverishment, or required impractical
changes in their education. We may
literally apply to her the old saying, "between two fires." On the one hand, she

was confronted by the spiritual sufferings of her husband, and his demand to have full freedom in carrying out his principles; on the other hand, she had to consult the happiness and welfare of her children, and consequently to acknowledge the impossibility of yielding to that demand. Between husband and wife an ever-widening discordance betrayed itself, and made itself felt in mutual recriminations as to the position each had taken up towards his creed, the one point on which there ever was the slightest disagreement or misunderstanding. The wife, at one moment, was disposed to appeal to the courts that the estate should be put under wardship, and the interests of the children be thus preserved. And when the Count proposed to make over all to her, she insisted on his giving her a formal deed, whereby all rights in his property, movable and immovable, should be conferred on her, with the exception of his later literary productions. These, as we know, are written for the express purpose of inculcating his creed, and the Count has, therefore, renounced all his rights in them, and they are public property, any one who chooses having the power to reprint them. Within the last few years, she has learned to look on his teaching more dispassionately, and has even trained herself to criticise it from an objective point of view. But I can best explain her actual state of mind by briefly summing up a conversation I had with her during my last visit in 1887.

So far from denying his doctrines in principle, she is, theoretically, in complete accord with them, and regards him as a man greatly in advance of his age. She, therefore, acknowledges his authority and reverences his ideal, but considers it would be unjust to cease to educate her younger children, as she was wont to educate the elder ones, so long as the new ideas of her husband on education continue to be unrecognised by society. In the same way, to divide their property among strangers, and to cast her children penniless on the world, when no one else is ready or willing to do the same, she not only considers impossible, but believes it to be her duty as mother to oppose any such scheme to the uttermost. When speaking to me on this subject, she exclaimed, with tears in her eyes, " It is hard for me now, since I have now to do all myself, whereas before I needed to be only his aid and helper. The education of the children, the care of the property, all has fallen on my shoulders. And then I am blamed for transgressing Christ's law of love and charity! As if I would not readily do all he wishes if I had no children; but he forgets all and everything for the sake of his creed." Nor was it only in reference to the question of education that she had to take a firm stand in opposition to her husband. A natural fear of the ill effect it might produce on the health of the children forced her to oppose him, when he desired that they, like himself, should observe a strict vegetarian diet.

As we might suppose, his views are differently judged by his children.

The eldest son, as far as I know, does not agree with the opinions of his father. When the latter surrendered all personal claims on his property, the son, in obedience to his mother's wish, undertook the management of the estate, and at the same time began his service in the chancery of the county zemstvo.

The second son expressed a wish to follow the rules laid down in his father's religious and social creed. He quitted the gymnasium, and three years ago, as I have been informed, married a young girl of twenty-two, with whom he settled on one of the smaller estates, and where, notwithstanding that his wife belongs to the higher

K

class of society, they lead a strictly simple life, and have no servants of any kind to aid them in keeping house.

The third son continued his course of education, but told me that he was perfectly in accord with his father as to the necessity of men leading a life of purity, and that he should do his best to observe the moral laws of the Count.

In general, I remarked in all the members of the family a desire to lead lives of the strictest simplicity, to make as little use as possible of the services of others, to help in every way the needy and suffering; and in all their acts they unostentatiously followed and adopted the teaching of their father.

But it is the second daughter more than all the rest who is devoted to her father, and, so far as is allowed her, she rigorously observes his every rule and maxim.

My younger sister, who spent her whole youth at Yásnaya Poliána, and now passes, together with her family, every summer

with the Countess, is also one of Leo
Nicholaevitch's sincerest admirers. But,
whilst she has a profound reverence for
the purity of his creed, and understands
the spirit of his teaching, she acknowledges
its lack of practicability, and is not afraid
openly to express her opinions. Leo
Nicholaevitch, in his turn, is wont to
answer her objections in that sarcastic
tone of his which, I may say, has replaced
the lively humour that formerly constituted
the great charm of his conversation. I
may, perhaps, be allowed to give a trifling,
but at the same time significant, example
of my sister's mocking attack, and the
quiet sarcasm with which it was parried.

In the olden days, Leo Nicholaevitch
was particularly fond of a certain sweet
dish, which we were accustomed to call
"ankovsky pie," after the name of the
good doctor who had given us the
recipe.

During my last visit I soon learned

that the term had assumed a different meaning, and that it was now employed by Leo Nicholaevitch, when he happened to be in a sarcastic mood, to express his discontent with us for undue hankering after comfort and luxury. I once happened to be with Leo Nicholaevitch whilst he was clearing up and dusting the things in his study. I helped him, and we had thoroughly swept the room out, and were standing on the balcony, brooms in hand, when my younger sister chanced to pass by. A little later, in presence of them all, she was laughingly congratulating me on my conversion, and declared she had never seen a more zealous disciple. She went on to relate how she saw me and the Count standing with brooms in hand, and how the latter made the sign of the cross over me, and, raising his eyes, solemnly asked me, "Dost thou renounce ankovsky pie and all its evil works?" upon which I as solemnly replied, "I do."

I also remember how, when we were getting ready to celebrate the twenty-fifth anniversary of the Count's marriage, he, evidently wishing to show his displeasure at the festivities with which we proposed to honour the event, inquired of us, "Is to-morrow really the jubilee of my wedding-day, or is it not rather the jubilee of ankovsky pie ?"

And now, in bringing my reminiscences of Count Tolstoy to an end, I purposely refrain from pronouncing any verdict of my own on his life or his teaching. I content myself with putting two questions that, no doubt, have already suggested themselves to the reader. Has Leo Nicholaevitch done all in his power to fulfil in his own life and conduct the rules he has laid down for others; and is he right to deprive his family of their claims to inherit his property ? For myself, I cannot imagine how any one, unless he be actuated by envy or malice, will venture to deny that, in every minutest point, he has, so far as was possible, practised in his life what he preaches in his books. To have deprived his children of their property would have been, probably, in the opinion of most men, an act of cruel and unjustifiable violence.

How far the teaching of Count Tolstoy is true appears to me to be a question that must be decided, not by us, but by posterity.

A LETTER

TO THE

WOMEN OF FRANCE

A LETTER

THE WORLD LIBRARY INS

TO THE

WOMEN OF FRANCE

ON "THE KREUTZER SONATA."

I.

INTRODUCTORY.

NOTHING is more difficult than to do good and at the same time to bring ill to no one.

In addressing this letter to you, I am actuated by this single desire, and shall be more than glad if I can, if only in part, attain that desire. It may be, the task is beyond my feeble power; but I shall be content if my letter affords you some moral satisfaction.

Let me at once come to the subject-matter of my letter.

The compositions of a great genius are like the sun that suddenly pours its full light into a dark place—at first our eyes are blinded with its dazzling rays, and we can see nothing.

So it was with Count Tolstoy's story, the "Kreutzer Sonata."

Most of the critics who have fallen foul of the novel are in exactly a like position to the bewildered inhabitants of a dark cave who have been startled by the sudden inburst of sunlight.

Some declare that they can see nothing because the sun shines too brightly: these are the critics who try to show that man is unfitted by nature to live singly and alone. Others affirm that it is impossible and dangerous to the sight to gaze on the sun: these are the critics who suppose that Tolstoy calls on us one and all to gaze straight on the sun instead of making a proper and reasonable use of its light, that is, as if he represented virginity to be universally compulsory. A third group of critics declare that men cannot avail themselves directly of the sunlight, but are obliged to have recourse to artificial light that flows from the natural light: these are the teachers of the Church, who assert that union in marriage is not only sinless but is recommended in the Gospels. And, lastly, we find critics who are in reality displeased at the light being introduced into dark places, merely because they are thus prevented from doing in the light what they were able to do with impunity in the darkness. Their opinion is at one with the belief of the ordinary reprobate, who jauntily assures us that men are endowed by nature with certain instincts, and that they have, in common with animals, the full sanction of nature to satisfy these desires. They thus decline to lay down any limit within which the passions of men should be confined. The only conclusion, therefore, that we can draw is that men in their relations to women are to have the same lawless liberty as is enjoyed by animals.

In a word, these critics, blinded by the light, have failed to seize the true meaning of Tolstoy's work, and have unwittingly attributed to him opinions directly the opposite to those which he in reality maintains.

On the contrary, women, with a keen presentiment that his work is a healthy and sound defence of their individual and social rights, have been able to keep themselves undazed by the new light which it throws upon the subject. They have been exhausted and worn out by the long struggle of ages to obtain their independence, and to secure their full protection against the coarse and sensual tyranny of men, that threatened in the end to crush their moral and physical strength. And if hitherto they have forborne to press their claims openly or in print, it is because they have long despaired of the appearance of a genius who would come to their aid with sufficient power to judge fairly this question of the rule of men over women, and pronounce a final and righteous verdict.

That decisive moment in the history of civilisation has now dawned. Count Tolstoy, whilst proclaiming woman's independence, has exposed the rude barbarous feeling by which men have always been guided, and still continue to be ruled, in their conduct and relation to women.

He has discovered the means by which, without violence or wrong to any one, the needful reform in our marriage laws and customs can be effected, and a complete but noiseless revolution be accomplished in the social and family life of Europe. And, when once this has been achieved, women will have the possibility of exercising their mild and useful activity in the different spheres of intellectual and moral labour.

But it may be asked, "Why have I not addressed this letter to my own country-women?"

There are two reasons. First, we do not enjoy full liberty of the press. This same novel, the "Kreutzer Sonata," was not published in Russian till the second year after it had been written. It has already made the round of the civilised world in Europe and America, during all which time it could circulate among our-selves only in manuscript, when, at last, the fame of its author and the success achieved by his novel were considered to justify its publication in Russia. But anything like a fair criticism of the work is for us all but impossible, and would be entirely use-less.

But I have a second and more urgent reason for addressing this letter to the women of France.

If this novel, the "Kreutzer Sonata," is destined to produce a radical reform in

our married and social life, and to secure
for women their rightful position in the
world, this reform will first be carried out
in France, because France has always been
the leading nation, and Frenchwomen the
leading women of Europe.

Nowhere has a tenderer sound and meaning been given to the word "mother" than
in France. French women always have
been and still are the lawgivers of fashion.
The women of no other country can rival
them in attractiveness and in grace. It is
in France that women have exercised the
greatest influence on the political life of a
people. At the same time, nowhere is the
law more stern or severe towards illegiti-
mate children, and nowhere has the increase
of population been brought to a lower rate.
In one word, the better the women of a
country are found to be, the more clearly
and the more sharply will their merits and
failings be brought out. It is in such a
country that the first reaction will take place

against actual family life and the actual position of women.

It is this that induces me to go over and review with you the grand truths enunciated by Count Tolstoy in the " Kreutzer Sonata " and in his " Post-prefatory Remarks " to the story.

In spite of its difficulties, I hope to accomplish the task I have set myself. From my twelfth year I have lived for a continuous number of summers with the author as a member of his family. I have thus been a witness of his family life, have seen how these ideas gradually grew upon him, and know the source and origin from which they sprang. Their gradual development, it is true, may be traced in his works, but they are mainly the necessary outcome of his own life.

In many of his tales he has sung the praises of family life. In one of his later productions, he has declared that woman's highest vocation is to give birth to, and to suckle children, that is, to be a mother. But in the "Kreutzer Sonata" he exalts the virgin above the mother. At first sight, these two views appear to be contradictory; but, in fact, they prove nothing more than a gradual and regular development in his thoughts and in his conception of the ideal. The seeming contradiction disappears directly we investigate and make ourselves acquainted with the real cause and reason of its composition.

The story is a revelation of the author's own experience. It is not the result of despair, or of disappointment at the failure of promised happiness; but it is the result of his experience of the fullest happiness family life can afford.

His experience has taught him its insufficiency to satisfy man's highest needs, and he therefore could not content himself with it, but sought out a new and higher form of happiness. The ordinary opinion that genius and talent are unfitted for the narrow circle

L

of family life is consequently once more proved to be erroneous; and, more than in anything else, Count Tolstoy has in this shown his originality and independence of mind and character. For herein lies the whole gist of the matter, that the composition of the " Kreutzer Sonata " is due to the happiness he has found in his family life.

He was, moreover, prompted to write it by that love for his neighbour which forms the guiding rule of his life, and which he has constantly set forth, not only in his writings, but in his daily practice and conduct.

Before entering on a critical analysis of the story, I ought perhaps to warn my readers that they are not justified in condemning the author for his sharp exposure of the shortcomings of women. These are to be regarded as the sad but natural result of the long-continued struggle between the two sexes, for which men, rather than women, are really answerable. Such,

at any rate, is evidently the view taken by
the author himself.

If this struggle has always existed and
is still going on, and if men have always
regarded, and still regard, women as mere
objects to satisfy their passions, the failings
and errors of men must always have been,
and will long continue to be, fatal to the
purity of family life, and to the true happiness of women in general.

An adequate solution of this question,
the restoration of women to their natural
rights, their emancipation from work that
is beyond their physical strength, and their
final rescue from the position of slaves to
the passions of men—all this has nothing
in common with the simpering flatteries
that are paid to women in drawing-rooms,
but constitutes the sole security and guarantee for the future weal, not only of women,
but of men themselves.

In the "Kreutzer Sonata" we have for
the first time a righteous solution of the

woman's question, and the definition of Christian marriage as deduced from the teaching of the Gospels. By making marriage Christian, we can alone escape the many evils and tragic horrors that now too often sully and poison our family life.

II.

HOW IS THE WOMAN'S QUESTION TO BE SOLVED?

In nothing, perhaps, does the history of the human race present such striking changes as in the position occupied by women at different periods and in different countries.

But just as we verify the temperature of the thermometer, so we may verify the degree to which sensuality prevails at any particular period. If we follow out the history of the woman's question, we shall see that the more sensualism obtains at any epoch, the worse will be the position of women at that time. For this reason, where polygamy prevails we find the despotism of man ; where polyandry prevails, we find woman supreme.

It is still within a comparatively recent date that widows were sacrificed in India to appease the spirits of their departed husbands, and new-born children were wont to be put to death in Northern Siberia, for no other reason than that it was considered a superfluous and embarrassing luxury to let them live. I myself, whilst occupying the post of examining magistrate in the Trans-Caucasus, had occasion some nine years ago to investigate several cases in which young girls had been violently carried off in order to compel them to conclude a forced marriage. This custom is still in force among those Georgian tribes who have been converted to the Christian faith.

It is not, however, of such races or tribes that I would speak now, but rather of what is done among the more polished peoples of the world, among those who boast of being the pioneers of civilisation. I have to speak of Christian Europe, where the equality of men and women is professed,

and where the woman has the right to with-
hold her consent to any proposal of marriage
that may be made to her.

But, in reality, according to the opinion
of Count Tolstoy, as expressed in the
"Kreutzer Sonata," European women are
in the position of degraded slaves, just because they are held by men to be nothing
more than the objects of sensual passion.

Throughout the story the author has
made Posdniescheff the spokesman and
mouthpiece of his ideas.

The story opens in a railroad carriage,
where the passengers have got into a chat
on the woman's question, and in the course
of the dispute the two extremest views
as to the rights of women are maintained.

First of all, we have the old merchant,
with his old-fashioned views about women.
He holds that the head of the house cannot
be called to account by the family for anything he does or says, and that he is

therefore free, notwithstanding any tie of marriage, to indulge in what revelry, and to form what connections he may think fit. From the wife he demands moral purity, and wifely obedience and fidelity. She must obey her husband implicitly, and, to secure such obedience, he recommends that she should be ruled with exemplary severity. He justifies his opinions by reminding us that Eve was created from one of Adam's ribs, and refers us to the words in the marriage-service, "the wife shall fear her husband." He winds up his argument by quoting the popular saying, "Do not trust your horse in the field, and do not trust your wife out of sight."

He is thus the exponent of what we call in Russia the patriarchal creed. It is plain that such a theory of the rights of men over women would reduce the latter to the grade of slaves.

A lawyer and his fellow-traveller, a lady, are the champions of the opposite creed, and they uphold the newer and more popular views on marriage. The former asserts that the right of divorce is not sufficiently extended in Russia; and his lady-friend declares that a woman should be guided exclusively by the feeling of love. The dress and manners of this lady, as well as her evidently close intimacy with the lawyer, proclaim her to be a thoroughly emancipated woman. From the tone of her speech we may conclude that she does not regard marriage as a sacrament, nor does she allow that marriage can have any other foundation than "true love;" and by this term she understands "the exclusive preference for one man or woman above all others."

The groundlessness of such a theory is at once exposed by the author, who makes the old merchant exclaim, "Ah, madam, all you say is not to the purpose. You forget that a law has been given to man."

And then the author introduces his hero,

Posdniescheff, who takes part in the dispute with the lawyer and his lady-friend, and shows them that such love can never serve as the basis of marriage, inasmuch as this is not love, but simply sexual attraction, that may be felt for any pretty woman or handsome man, and which consequently cannot be felt throughout life for one and the same person.

The discussion soon comes to an end, and Posdniescheff is left alone with the supposed narrator of the tale.

He tells him the whole story of his life, explains his earlier ideas of and relation to women, and describes all the tragic circumstances connected with the murder of his unhappy wife. In the course of his narrative, he criticises and condemns the present position of women, the modern conception of marriage, and finally sets forth his own views and ideas on these two questions of the day.

"If the story is to be told, it must be

told from the beginning," says Posdniescheff;
and he commences to relate what kind of
life our young men are wont to lead before
their marriage.

In this way Posdniescheff systematically
works out his thesis, that in Europe men
have degraded women to a state of slavery,
merely to satisfy their own passions. The
equality, of which we talk so loudly and
write so fluently, does not really exist, and
we only lie when we declare women to be
free and to have the same rights as men.

He begins by describing his own life.
" I lived up to my marriage," he says, "as
others lived, that is, I led an immoral life ;
but all the time I was convinced that I was
living as I ought to live."

Consequently, the life of Posdniescheff is
to be accepted as the model by which all
men live, and they are all convinced that
such a life is regular and correct.

Posdniescheff lost his purity when he was
fifteen. But before that he had been cor-

rupted in mind and corrupted in deed, since "his very abstentions were impure." "Women were to him a sweet forbidden fruit, and his desires gave him no rest."

He suffered from and struggled against these desires. At last, one of his companions took him to a house, "where he fell," and ceased to be any longer pure.

But we must not condemn the young lad because he fell. He had suffered much and struggled hard ; and his fall filled him with horror. Nothing can be more truthful or more touching than the language in which he describes his grief at the bitter thought of his moral degradation :—

" I remember how at once, even there, before I had left the room, I was filled with grief, with such grief that I longed to weep, to weep for the loss of my purity, for the irrevocable change that had henceforth come over my relationship to women. I could no

longer be to them, they could no longer
be to me as before."

He sinned as all his young friends had
sinned. He had been led away under the
influence of the circle in which he lived
and moved. On this point Posdniescheff
speaks out with his usual blunt clearness:

"The fact is that, in my case, as in the
case of nine-tenths, if not more, not only
of our class, but of the whole people, even
the peasantry included, the horrible thing
was that I had not fallen a victim to the
seductive charms of one particular woman:
no, it was not any woman who had seduced
me; but I fell because those who surrounded me looked upon what in reality
was a sin as something perfectly lawful,
something necessary for my health, or, at
the worst, as a very natural and pardonable distraction in a young man."

And so all our young men, with very
few exceptions, have ceased to be pure
in body before they marry. In the mean-

time a girl is expected to remain pure. She must be chaste and innocent up to the date of her marriage.

But why is this difference made between a young man and a young girl? Is not a woman as jealous as a man of her future partner for life? If it is so necessary for the man, whose life is already sullied and corrupt, that his wife should be innocent and chaste, why is it not equally, and even more, necessary for a woman whose life is still pure, that her husband should be alike pure and of unblemished reputation?

But it is not with merely one offence against morality that most men have to accuse themselves. And Posdniescheff frankly confesses this :—

"I avoided those women who, by the birth of a child or by their attachment to me, might in any way try to bind me. For all I know, there may have been children, and there may have been sincere attach-

ment, but I always acted as if there were
neither the one nor the other. And I not
only counted such conduct to be thoroughly
honourable, but I was proud of it. And
this is the blackguardism of the whole affair.
The depravity is not in anything physical;
it is not in the debasement of the body
that the depravity consists; but the depravity, the real depravity, consists in the
denial of all moral obligations to the woman
with whom we have been on the most
intimate terms. And I considered it a
duty to make myself thus free. I remember
how terribly I once felt ashamed because
I could not pay a woman who, it may be,
loved me, and who, at any rate, had given
herself to me, and how I only regained
my peace of mind when I had sent her
some money, and thereby given her to
understand that I did not consider myself
under any further obligation to her."

In these words there is a profound truth,
whether we choose to recognise it or not.

For no one ever blames a man for freeing himself from the moral obligation arising from his intimate connection with a woman. He buys his freedom with money. Of course it is easier for him to find money than it is for the woman, seeing that nearly all the spheres of industry are open to him and closed to her. And in this resides their inequality. He knowingly and placidly resigns himself to the moral ruin of the woman who has sacrificed herself to his pleasure, and risked for him the loss of all that is most precious to her.

We naturally ask, why do the same acts that bring no shame to the man involve the woman in lasting shame and in disgrace that can never be wiped out? Why is not the same law applied equally to both?

But this is not all. The question is not so much about the man, who easily and without loss of character frees himself from all moral responsibility. The real question

is, what is to become of the woman, who has
to bear the whole fault, and on whom alone
the shame falls.

Is it convenient or necessary that I
should speak here of prostitution? All the
horror of this evil, which, it would seem,
has taken deepest root in civilised Europe,
is too patent to require to be pointed out.
Count Tolstoy, better than elsewhere, has
alluded to this subject in his " Post-prefatory
Remarks" :—

"It cannot be right that certain people
should be allowed, on the plea that it is
necessary for their health, to destroy others,
body and soul, any more than we should
think of allowing a privileged class to drink
the blood of their poorer neighbours on
the pretext that it was necessary for their
health."

But is there really any great difference
between the position assigned to these
wretched creatures and that forced on the
woman who has once fallen? With what

M

shame is she banned from society, and left to bear alone the consequences of her weakness in yielding to a passionate impulse, left alone with the money, by means of which the man, her seducer, becomes free of her and free from all responsibility and obligation?

And all this flagrant injustice is generally justified on the plea that man's nature is such that he absolutely needs this distraction, and that to deny it to him would involve the ruin of his bodily health. The prime upholders of this opinion, according to Posdniescheff, are our doctors. Thanks to them, the idea has become so universally accepted, that even mothers consider it well to tacitly encourage their sons when they begin to lead such a life, and our municipalities take care that convenient houses of debauchery are provided for them.

I do not find it necessary to dwell upon this question. I believe with Count Tolstoy

that "temperate restraint is less dangerous
and less injurious to the health than incon-
tinency, and that we can find around us
examples, however few in number, to prove
our case."

For this our doctors cannot be too
severely censured. How few of them ever
think of busying themselves with insisting
on the observance of those hygienic and
sanitary rules in our family life which
would obviate the dangers and temptations
that now beset young people. A doctor
is attached to each of our educational
establishments, but in which of them are
our youths, much less our girls, taught any
of those lessons of physiology which would
give them the necessary knowledge to
escape evils into which they now fall
through ignorance and thoughtlessness?

Further on I shall have occasion to
quote Posdniescheff on the importance of
hygiene and a scientific education in the
due ordering of family life. By a proper

attention to these two conditions we can easily ensure continency in our youths, without risking any danger to their health, and thus shield them from vice and shame.

But if the belief that men's health can be preserved only at the expense of women were to a certain degree well founded, we should be confronted with an awkward dilemma. Either a small number of men must be physically ruined, owing to their forced continency, or a large number of women must be ruined, both physically and morally. It is hard to believe that this can be a law of nature. I am convinced that the question would long ago have been settled in the sense Count Tolstoy has solved it, if it had not been for the immoral support given to the opinion by society and the doctors. Once more I quote the words of Posdniescheff : " What in reality is a sin is regarded, at the worst, as a very natural and pardonable distraction in a young man." Ask any man to tell you conscientiously and frankly how men speak and think of women. Of what is their confidential chat made up beyond cynical witticisms, inuendos, and jokes at the expense of women? Count Tolstoy has not failed to notice this common trait, as when in the railroad carriage the merchant, already an old man, laughingly whispered in the ear of the clerk the story of one of his love adventures.

There are many who propose early marriages as the surest means of preserving social morality, but at the same time they are obliged to admit the inconvenience of such marriages from a material point of view.

But here again we are met with a difficulty. We must either put up with the inadequacy of our pecuniary means, or reconcile ourselves to the unchecked prevalence of immorality, and to the further degradation of women. If the rich man,

under the pretence of preserving the health
of his sons, causes the ruin of several
women, their ruin, in its turn, will have
a disastrous effect on his sons and their
descendants.   For it surely is not necessary
to prove that immorality invariably leaves
its indelible traces, and not seldom leads
to crime.

The genius and originality of Count
Tolstoy are conclusively shown in those
portions of his tale in which he dissects and
analyses the actual position girls are made
to occupy in contemporary society.   He
has thrown such light on to this dark
spot in our social organisation, that not a
single critic has ventured to question his
facts or dispute his conclusions.

In modern society women lay themselves
out and are eager to become the slaves of
men's sensual passions.   It is in reference
to this that Posdniescheff directs our attention to the defective and dishonest character
of the education we give our daughters.

Under the pretext of preserving their innocence, we carefully conceal from them all
knowledge of the lives their husbands were
wont to lead up to the time of their marriage.

"In nearly every romance the feelings
of the hero are portrayed in detail, the
ponds and copses round which he walks
in pensive thought are described, but, whilst
dwelling on his great love for the heroine,
the novelist tells us nothing about the life
he led before, nor is there a word said of
his visits to certain disreputable houses, or
his gay adventures with ladies'-maids, cooks,
and strange women. Or if there be such
indelicate novels, where we are told all
this, the greatest care is taken to keep
them out of the hands of those to whom
such knowledge is most necessary — unmarried girls. And they are so well trained
in this hypocrisy, that at last, like the
English, they begin actually to believe that
we are all moral people, and that we live
in a moral world."

Most, probably many, of my readers will not agree that we ought to let young unmarried women know anything of the darker side of human life. But I hope that this letter may induce them to prefer the lesser evil—a knowledge of the truth —to the still greater evil that later awaits unmarried women—when they are awakened from their illusion.

Posdniescheff's indignation is further, and with perfect justice, aroused against men when they come into society in order to look around them and choose a bride. With his habitual frankness he confesses what his conduct was :—

"I wallowed in every dissipation of the lowest kind, and at the same time was busy seeking out a girl whose purity of mind should make her worthy to be my bride. Many I rejected, simply because their moral reputation was not sufficiently good to justify me in marrying them."

And this is the conclusion to which he comes :—

"This is what ought to happen, when a gentleman of this kind approaches my sister or daughter at a ball, I, knowing the life he leads, ought to go up to him, take him aside, and quietly say, " My dear fellow, you forget, I know, how you live, where you pass your nights, and with whom. This is no place for you. The girls here are pure and innocent. Go elsewhere." This is what I ought to do and say ; but, as it is, when the gentleman appears, dances with my sister or daughter, and puts his arm round her waist, I rub my hands with joy, as I think how well connected and how rich he is."

The recollections of the ball fill up the cup of Posdniescheff's indignation :—

"The girls sit in a row, and the men, as if they were at a slave-mart, stroll round, and inspect what is on sale. They walk up and down, smirking with pleasure to think that all has been so admirably arranged for them."

And, in truth, the right to invite the girl to dance belongs to the man; and to the man belongs the right to take the initiative step in choosing a bride. But, at this point, Posdniescheff's companion, who had hitherto seemed to agree with all he said, was roused to exclaim somewhat testily, "Well, and how can it be otherwise? Would you, then, have women make the proposal of marriage?" And not a few of my fair readers will in the same way cry out, "What a horrible idea!"

But it evidently is not the idea of granting to woman the right to choose husbands for themselves that is horrible; but what is horrible is the startling plainness with which Count Tolstoy put the truth before us. Once more we see what a light he throws on the dark ways of society, and how thorough is his exposure of the hypocrisies and pretences of a debauched world.

Which, after all, is worse and more immoral—that an experienced and arrant rake should choose for himself from among pure and innocent girls a rich and beautiful bride, or that a pure-minded girl should openly avow her affection for the man to whom she is willing to give her hand, especially when her choice' is made from among youths who have led lives as stainless as her own?

But why does a man demand that the woman he makes his wife should be pure in mind and body? If it is on the broad principle that we ought all to be pure in life, that is all Count Tolstoy insists on. But we know that this requirement of morality is made by the man and refused to the woman. And this is, if I may use the expression, the very gastronomy of debauchery.

We must not, however, suppose that Count Tolstoy recognises the right of women to make the proposal of marriage. And if he has alluded to the subject at all, it is only as an additional proof of the existing inequality of the sexes.

No one, of course, will deny that man is superior to woman in physical strength. It is for this reason that our social organisation, social customs, and social principles have been developed rather under the influence of man than under that of woman. To this he owes his pre-eminence and those numerous laws of society which humour and satisfy his sensual desires and instincts.

Posdniescheff shows most clearly that it is the bodily charms and attractions of a woman that mainly interest a man both before and after his marriage. However galling this may be to us all, and however reluctant we may be to admit it, this is the simple truth and fact. Nor can it be otherwise, so long as the carnal pleasures of men are as varied as those in which men of modern society indulge, at least up to the time of their marriage. And the like phenomenon is to be remarked among our fallen women.

"We all know," Posdniescheff exclaims, "the estimate men form of women. 'Wein, Weib, und Gesang' is the favourite refrain of all poets and singers."

And this low estimate of women, as expressed in the German song, is encouraged and approved by women themselves. This is the natural result of the education they receive, and Posdniescheff shrewdly exposes the tricks of coquetry they are taught to practise :—

"Mothers know what men really are, they learn it from their husbands, and know it only too well. But, whilst they pretend to believe in the purity of men, they act as if they really believed the contrary. They know with what bait men are to be caught for their daughters. It is only we men who are so innocently ignorant, and we are ignorant because we find it convenient to be so; but women know very well that the most exalted poetical love, as we like to call it, will be blind to moral worth, and is mainly excited by physical beauty and by the adventitious attractions of a woman's head-dress, the colour and fashion of her dress. Ask a practised coquette which of these two dangers she would prefer to risk, to appear in the presence of her suitor convicted of a flagrant falsehood, heartless conduct, even some act of moral turpitude, or to come before him in an ugly ill-made dress, and there is not one of her class who will not choose the first. She understands that when her noble suitor gets eloquent about the moral virtues, it is mere talk; what attracts him are her bodily charms, and to become their possessor he is ready to pardon any slips in morality; but there is one thing no suitor will forgive, and that is a tasteless ill-fashioned abortion of a dress. A coquette knows this from experience; an innocent girl knows it instinctively, in the same way as animals know it."

And I would venture to ask, Why is it that most of us only care to marry good looks and handsome faces? How many girls there are, whom we cannot call pretty, but who are endowed with excellent hearts and lofty minds, and how politely we men cut them!

It is not then surprising if dress plays the chief part in a woman's life. The natural object of dress is to protect the body from the weather; but its proper use is entirely ignored and quite forgotten by the followers of fashion.

"This is why women," Posdniescheff petulantly exclaims, "wear those abominable jerseys and detestable tournures, and why they go about with bare shoulders, naked arms, and exposed breasts. Women, especially those who know what men are, understand perfectly well what value they are to give to their loud talk about virtue and modesty, and experience has taught them that the only thing men care about is the body, and whatever sets it off in a false but attractive form ; and they humour their tastes."

For my own part, I am inclined to criticise present fashions exclusively from a hygienic point of view, and I think it is only fair to remember that the doctors, whom Posdniescheff condemns so harshly, being mere caterers to women's fancies and caprices, have long vainly protested against stays, high-heeled boots, garters, long trains, and other deformities of modern fashion. I would add that of late attention has been turned to the weight of a woman's dress, and it has been found that the average weight exceeds that of a man's suit.

No one, I suppose, will dispute that the dresses now in fashion are uncomfortable and injurious to the wearer. And all this inconvenience is endured for the sake of outward look and show. Many pay still more dearly for external appearance. But the low dresses in which women are pleased

to flaunt their immodesty are an unanswer-
able proof that Count Tolstoy is not far
wrong when he asserts that women dress
solely to tempt men by showing off their
bodily charms.

This is what Posdniescheff has to say on
the subject :—

"Even in earlier days I felt awkward and
confused when I saw a lady in a full ball-
dress ; but now the sight is something
terrible, something dangerous to people
and contrary to the law, and I am always
inclined to call for the police, summon protection against the danger, and demand that
the dangerous object should be got rid of
and turned out as speedily as possible."

I should like to ask a mother how she
felt the first time she was compelled to put
on a low dress, and how she feels now when
she forces her daughter to wear such a
dress. She naturally felt the dress to be
an offence against womanly modesty. But
if then she wept tears of shame, what is

N

it she now whispers into her daughter's ear? " Never mind ; you will get used to it. Every woman dresses like that now, and you do not know how it pleases the men."

The only conclusion we can draw from the inquiry we have just made as to the kind of life led by the greater number of our young men and women before marriage is, that modern society has been organised with one single aim—to satisfy the sexual passions of men. The consequence is, these passions are more and more developed, and we have so managed things that, as Posdniescheff justly remarks, "from the highest work of art down to the trumpery picture on a match-box," all is so got up as to pander to the lower instincts of man's nature.

All this tends to humiliate and weaken women. We must, therefore, all the more admire the constant efforts made by women to acquire a footing in different spheres of activity, without abandoning their immediate home duties, and the success with which those efforts have been attended.

The increased activity of women has, however, produced a corresponding laxity in work on the part of men, though to labour in the sweat of his brow is the original command laid on man. They have grown effeminate and lackadaisical through long abandonment to their favourite vices. With an easy conscience they continue to take advantage of the immunity afforded them by the unjust bearing of the laws of inheritance on women. They are twenty times stronger than women, and more capable of physical labour; but they have succeeded in usurping to themselves the administration of affairs, and have made their position a means of exploiting women. We have only to turn to France, and ask ourselves who are the principal monopolists, even in branches of industry for which women are especially suited, to

be convinced that men form the large
majority of this privileged class.

Indeed, most of us admit that the position
occupied by women is nujust and unfair.
But we are satisfied with having made the
admission.   Little or nothing has been
done by the law-giver or by society to
ameliorate the wrong.

The ordinary and popular view of the
rights and true position of women, the
representatives of which in the "Kreutzer
Sonata" are the lawyer and his lady friend,
is essentially dishonest and immoral.   Without taking a single step to redress the
vexations and humiliating restrictions we
have imposed on women, the upholders
of this view noisily proclaim the equality
of men and women, and are never tired
of crying out, "We must educate our
women.   We must give them political
rights.   Women are no longer slaves, but
are free."

They act, in short, like the man who

dangles a piece of meat before the mouth of a starving creature, and then, instead of giving it to him, complacently swallows it himself.

It is cruel hypocrisy and mere cant to propose these rights to women, unless at the same time we afford them the means of exercising them.

In fact, women are offered the right to compete with men in the different branches of labour, but all the while have to bear, give birth to, and suckle children, and have to suffer from the injustice of the laws of inheritance.

There is no doubt that when these men proclaim the equality of women, they adopt the cry as a convenient means of maintaining man's pre-eminence over woman.

"We talk," says Posdniescheff, "about the new education of women; but it is all talk. The education women now receive is exactly what it should be, so long as we keep true to our present opinion of women, in which, at least, we are honest and sincere. The education of women always corresponds with the opinion men form of them. Take all our poems, paintings, statues, beginning with our love songs, and naked Venuses or Phrynes, and we see how women are considered to be nothing more than toys of men's pleasures. It is the fashion now to declare that we respect woman, because we give up to her our place in an omnibus, or pick up her handkerchief if she lets it fall; and some of us go so far as to maintain that she has a right to occupy any public post and to take her place in a government bureau. We talk in this way, but we keep to our old estimate of women, and she remains a pretty toy to amuse ourselves with. And women know this, and feel that they are slaves. The mere fact that we make no scruple to treat them as convenient objects of our lust is sufficient to prove the slavery of women. We are ready to emancipate them, to give them

all kinds of rights, make them in name
our equals ; but we continue to regard them
as before, and bring them up in such a
way that they can play the part at home
and in society. And so, women remain
humiliated corrupted slaves, and men remain lewd corrupted slaveholders. No
higher classes, no gymnasia, no courses
can change this. A change in their position
can be effected only by a change in the
way men look on women, and in the way
women look on themselves. As it is, the
ideal of every girl, however brilliantly
educated she may be, is to attract the
largest number of men. She may be well
versed in mathematics, and another may
be an admirable musician; but this will
make no difference. The only lesson a
woman really cares about learning is how
to fascinate men."

Putting aside the false character of this
pretended equality, it has in many cases
led to the fatal result of allowing men full

freedom to indulge in debauchery, and affording women a like undesirable liberty. Of this we have an example in the lawyer's lady-friend, and a proof in the opinions she maintains.

Reverence for marriage as a sacrament has thus disappeared from among us, together with other venerable beliefs and customs of the old patriarchal times.

It is not easy to over-estimate the service Count Tolstoy has rendered in discovering a just solution of the woman's question. He puts the old ideas of the open slavery of women, which the merchant admires, and defends with such warmth, in opposition to the newer ideas of our social reformers, who, however, have nothing better to offer women than a fictitious freedom, and whose ideas, if carried out, must contribute to the spread of social demoralisation. He condemns alike the slavery of women as it existed in the olden times, and the immorality that is engendered by more modern

ideas, and shows how, in both cases, the
degradation of woman is the necessary consequence. The equality of men and women
for which he pleads consists in the elevation
of men to that level of purity which men
still require and exact from the women they
choose for their wives.

"The slavery of women," says Posdniescheff, "does not consist in the denial of
their right to give a vote, or to fill the
post of magistrate—such privileges confer
no rights—but it consists in their enjoying
the same freedom as men enjoy; the right
to refuse to be the puppet of man's animal
desires just as often and just when he
chooses; the right to choose for herself
the man she wishes to make her husband,
instead of being chosen. You will say,
that would be indecent and unbecoming.
Well, then, do not give these indecent and
unbecoming rights to men. As it is, you
deprive women of the right you confer on
men."

Count Tolstoy, it will be seen, proposes, not to give women the right of choosing partners for life, but to deprive men of the right. He speaks more fully of this in the eighth chapter of his story, when Posdniescheff angrily declaims against this right being conferred exclusively on men. "If we found," he says, "the old Russian custom of employing professional match-makers to be degrading, our present mode of arranging marriages is a thousand times more degrading. At any rate, under the old system, the chances for both were equal."

Without dwelling on the question how marriage should be concluded, and without expressing any positive opinion on the subject, Count Tolstoy makes it an absolute condition of marriage that the bridegroom should have led a pure life up to the time of marriage, and should afterwards cleave to one woman.

Only then, when the wife ceases to be

the puppet of man's passion, can she hope to breathe freely and to enjoy true liberty. Only then can her mental and moral powers be legitimately developed, because only then will she have the possibility of profiting by education, by the political rights that may be given her, and by the profession or occupation she chooses to adopt. Only then will she be really placed on an equal footing with her husband.

Posdniescheff is quite right when he declares that under the actual order of things such equality does not exist.

"Tell any mother," he says, "or any girl, the truth, namely, that the whole occupation of her life is, and must be, to catch men, and she, of course, will be offended. But this is the be-all and end-all of her existence. And what is most horrible is when we see poor young innocent girls engaged in this chase after men."

Having in this way solved the woman's question, Count Tolstoy proceeds with his usual clearness of argument and brilliancy of illustration to discuss the consequences of woman's enslavement.

We cannot enslave an animal, much less a human being, except against the will of the creature or individual enslaved. If I were to give an historical sketch of the position occupied by women at different epochs and in different countries, we should see that throughout there has been a struggle, and that the struggle is still going on. There have been instances when the all but complete extermination of women has marked their revolt against the tyrannous and cruel unsurpation of authority by men. Sometimes, but rarely, victory has remained on the side of women. The struggle as carried on in our own days is naturally of a milder character.

Posdniescheff warns us how women "play

on the sensual feelings of man, and in
this way so completely subdue him that,
whilst in form he chooses one of them
as his bride, in reality it is the bride who
chooses him. And once having obtained
this influence over him, women begin to
make an ill use of their advantage, and
end by easily securing power over men
in general."

If we study the history and organisation
of polygamy, we invariably find that it is
based on an excessive culture of all that
is tender and delicate in woman. For this
purpose a life of idle inactivity is adopted,
as well as a luxurious table, costly furnished
houses, and elaborate dresses. And these
are exactly what the women of our day
most hanker after. By making them the
principal pursuit of their existence, women
have made themselves the slaves of men
in all the economical relations of life.

Posdniescheff gives us the explanation
of this when he says, " Go into the shops

of any of our larger towns. In these shops you will find goods worth millions; but, instead of trying to value the products of human labour that are stored up in there, look and see if in one shop out of ten there is a single article for men's use. All the luxuries of life are used by women, and it is they who keep up the demand for them. Count over our factories. The larger number of them produce useless ornaments, carriages, furniture, jewellery for women. Millions of people and whole generations of slaves wear their lives out in convict labour in our factories to supply the fancies of women, who, like empresses, keep in slavery and hard work nine-tenths of the human race; and all because women have been degraded and deprived of equal rights with men. And they take their revenge on us, and deftly catch us in their nets."

There can be no occasion to show that in such a condition of things it is ridiculous to expect that the intellectual and physical powers of women or of men will be properly and fully developed.

The consequences of the enslavement of women are not less grave in their reaction on the relation between husband and wife, and parents and children. It is not easy to imagine anything more touching or more instructive than the story of Posdniescheff's married life. In this portion of his narrative he does not try to hide anything or to make excuses for himself, but is perfectly open and frank. At the time he was quarrelling with his wife he imagined that these disagreements were peculiar to them, and never disturbed the peace of other homes. But later experience discovered to him that similar scenes occur in every family. "For a time I was tortured with the thought that it was only I who lived so badly and so differently to what I had expected with my wife, and that quarrels like ours never took place in other families. I did not then know that it was the fate common to us all." And thus the life of Posdniescheff and his wife is but an example of ordinary life. And the source and cause of the misunderstandings and disputes that arose between the two was nothing else than the enslavement and inferior position of the wife.

If what has been just said concerning the false relation in which women stand to men be true, it is evident that Posdniescheff, whilst imagining it was her mind and heart and soul that attracted him, in reality loved his wife for her outward bodily charms. His was what we call a marriage of love; but his love was essentially sensual, with a slight mixture of poetical sentiment to give it a proper colouring. What he sought in marriage was the satisfaction of his desires. In the meantime, his wife in her innocence sought something higher and purer in marriage.

Posdniescheff justly attributes all these

quarrels to the difference in feeling and
sentiment which, on the very first day of
marriage, a pure wife will experience, in
opposition to the man, who does his best
to juggle himself into the belief that he is
moved, not by sensual desire, but by love.
We must not forget that Posdniescheff himself has told us how he felt on the night
when he first fell. But, under the influence
of passion, he forgets that his wife will be
tortured by a feeling like to that from which
he himself then suffered. It is consequently
in vain that he expects from her a passion,
of which her as yet pure nature makes her
feel ashamed.

Such was the origin of the discord that
sprang up between the two, but, as Posdniescheff reminds us, it became the more intense
in proportion as their mutual sensual passion grew in force.

"The novelty of love was already spent
when it had already received its satisfaction, and we remained in our real relation

o

one to the other, that is to say, we were
two egoists, each desirous to get from the
other the fullest possible amount of pleasure.
I used to wonder why there was this constant feeling of irritated antagonism between
us, but now it is plain and patent to me:
it was nothing else than the protest of our
human nature against our animal nature,
which had got the mastery of us."

We need seek no other reason for the
quarrels between Posdniescheff and his wife.
There was no *mésalliance* in their marriage;
they were both wealthy, and belonged to
the same class of society. Posdniescheff had
married "from love, and not for money."
He had resolved to lead a moral life after
his marriage, and even in his youth was
often ridiculed by his comrades because
his conduct was less irregular than theirs. It
is plain that Count Tolstoy had purposely
surrounded the marriage of his hero with
every outwardly favourable circumstance, to
make us feel the more strongly that it

was nothing else than an undue abandonment to sensuality, the crowning characteristic of contemporary life, that brought misery into their homes, and finally led Posdniescheff himself to commit the most horrible of crimes.

It is this same sensual feeling that before long engendered jealousy. But Posdniescheff's jealousy is not so much the outcome of his natural disposition as the result of the education that had been given to the wife, in common with all women of our day.

She had been educated in accordance with the "requirements of the position occupied by women in our society." She, therefore, believed her whole worth to reside in physical beauty. To preserve that beauty, she first refused to suckle her children, and then had recourse to artificial means to prevent her again becoming a mother.

At a first glance, we might be tempted

to think this would serve to foster the sensual attachment of a husband. But Posdniescheff, with marvellous simplicity and clearness, points out how completely this excited within him a feeling of jealousy.

"When I saw how lightly she freed herself from the moral responsibility of a mother, I very justly, though unconsciously, concluded that she might, with like ease, free herself from wifely responsibility."

Under such circumstances there could be no trust or faith between the two. And the absence of all trust completed the discord. But Count Tolstoy does not represent Posdniescheff as being unfaithful to his marriage vow. He only hints at the possibility, and even more than possibility, that such would be the case. And this possibility arises from the same cause, the enslavement of woman, which prevents her from being a wife-companion, and makes her only a wife-concubine. Posdniescheft very well explains this, when he is drawing for us the portrait of Trouacheffsky :—

"He was a pitiful fellow. There was nothing manly in him, at least in my eyes, and as I estimated him. I do not say this because he played an important part in my family life, but because he really was such as I describe him. Besides, the fact that there was nothing in him only proves how unexacting my wife was. If it had not been he, it would have been some one else."

In all and in everything we recognise the harmful results of the humiliating position to which we have reduced women, involving as it does an unnatural eagerness on their part to avoid, at any cost, whatever may cause them pain or grief. Take but one instance. We have all agreed to declare that children are a joy and a blessing sent by God, yet, as Posdniescheff reminds us, among the higher classes of society, "children are a plague and a torment, and nothing else. Ask mothers in our class of society, and there is scarcely one among them who will not tell you that, from the fear lest their children should fall ill and die, they would prefer to have had none; nor will they suckle their babe lest they should become too attached to it and suffer too terribly from its loss. That is, these women do not sacrifice themselves for any beloved object, but are ready to sacrifice the beloved object, to save themselves pain and sorrow."

In measure as Count Tolstoy, in the course of his story, reveals the existing struggle between man and woman, the moral enslavement of the latter, and the economical enslavement of the former, the feeling it produces on the mind of his reader becomes intenser and more sad.

Why this mutual enslavement of one another? And why this revelation of the sores of modern society? Is not the writer `after all only adding fuel to the flame ?

There is but one answer to questions like these. The struggle is so patent and undoubted, and its consequences are so terrible and injurious, that it is a duty to tell the truth, and if possible, uproot and destroy the evil.

In what were the Posdniescheffs guilty ? They had both indulged in dreams of a happy family life. And yet, she meets with a horrible death, and his whole life is wrecked and ruined. Were they, then, both unworthy of having their dream of happiness realised ?

But sensuality has taken a deep root throughout the civilised world. It has poisoned our ideas of honour. How often we hear of mere youths challenging one another to mortal duel for the sake of a girl, to whom they have both paid their addresses, and who, in most cases, is equally indifferent to one and the other?

Nothing but a radically false idea of honour could have made us accept for sacred the rule that, if a wife betrays her husband, the latter must wipe out the disgrace in blood. And the woman? What part does she play in this last scene of the family drama? Though the guilty cause of the whole tragedy, she quietly keeps aloof, and no one expects that she should do otherwise. From her the world only demands personal beauty. And he who proves the boldest and most cunning can possess that beauty.

Need we be surprised, then, if the moral development of women being thus checked and thwarted, their only possible mission, as society is now constituted, is "to hinder and shackle the progress of humanity in its struggle towards truth and happiness?"

All this will continue so long as woman herself does not recognise the evil, and does not herself strive to weaken the power of sensuality over men. She alone can act as mother and as wife. And she alone is able to save him from being inveigled by those charms of which she is the sole possessor and disposer.

WHAT IS CHRISTIAN MARRIAGE?

IT cannot be denied that ecclesiastical marriages are gradually diminishing in number. In Western Europe civil marriages are in habitual use. According to statistics, the number of divorces in countries professing the Christian faith amounts to 43,000 a year. Of these, 23,000 are to be assigned to America. We must not forget that among Catholics divorce is not allowed. We can, therefore, form a tolerably distinct idea of the actual state of married life. In Russia, also, we remark a decrease in the number of ecclesiastical marriages.

" But with us," says Posdniescheff in reference to the steps generally taken preparatory to marriage, "out of ten who marry it is

certain that nine have no belief in marriage
as a sacrament, and do not even believe that
the ceremony in which they are taking part
imposes any obligation on them. And when
out of a hundred men there is scarcely one
who in the strict sense of the word is not
already married, and out of fifty perhaps one
who has not determined beforehand to betray
his wife at the first convenient opportunity,
when the majority of men look upon marriage
as a formality, the observance of which gives
right to the possession of a certain woman,
only think what a terrible significance all
this gives to marriage."

Consequently, neither religion, nor habitua-
tion to one's wife nor children, have proved
to have sufficient force to preserve the sacred-
ness of marriage. And this involves the
decadence of family life, the best and surest
guarantee of social prosperity and order.
For sad as are the surroundings of modern
married life, we have proofs that the moral
influence of the family is as necessary as

ever. Statistics teach us that bachelors form the principal contingent of suicides.

Count Tolstoy, whilst insisting so earnestly on the degraded position of women, and the struggle going on between the two sexes in Europe, takes care to point out at least one of the remoter causes of the evil.

He finds that the cause lies in the erroneous doctrines held by the Churches on marriage.

The Churches teach that marriage is a state of perfection not inferior to that of monasticism, and that marriage was founded by Christ. In opposition to this doctrine, Count Tolstoy writes in his "Post-prefatory Remarks," "Christ established no institutions, and never instituted marriage." To support this opinion, he quotes numerous texts from the gospels, the principal being the verses he has selected as a motto for his story. "But I say unto you, That whosoever looketh on a woman to lust after her hath committed adultery with her already in his heart." "His disciples say unto Him, If the case of the man be so with his wife, it is not good to marry. But He said unto them, All men cannot receive this saying, save they to whom it is given." The other texts which he quotes are, Matt. v. 28, 29, 31, 32 ; xix. 8 ; and xix. 10–12, to which I accordingly refer my readers.

The conclusion drawn from these texts is that Christ held up virginity as an ideal for our guidance, but that He did not institute marriage. He holds that the teaching of the Churches is at variance with the gospels, inasmuch as they acknowledge cohabitation in marriage to be sinless, and to a certain extent obligatory, since our courts of law regard physical debility as an adequate ground for divorce.

Most probably some of my readers will cry out with the critics, " Then Count Tolstoy teaches and recommends celibacy."

Count Tolstoy understands by celibacy

the ideal of that chastity which Christ recommended for our guidance. But neither he nor any one else pretends that it should be universally practised in life, and Christ Himself has said, "All men cannot receive this saying."

But it will be asked, What is marriage according to the teaching of Count Tolstoy? Basing his doctrine on the spiritual teaching of the Gospel, he gives no exact definition of marriage, but for all practical purposes of human life he understands by marriage monogamy. Thus, there is no outward difference between marriage as interpreted by the Churches, and marriage as understood by Tolstoy. But, on the other hand, the spiritual distinction is enormous. The difference consists in chastity, as recommended by Christ, being proposed as an ideal to all of us, married or unmarried, in teaching that aspiration towards such an ideal sanctifies life in general, and therefore also married life. The married, according to the teaching of Tolstoy, do not look on the intimate relation between man and wife as the Churches look on it. Regarding the satisfaction of passion, even in marriage, as a sin, an offence, an almost unavoidable evil, they can continually aspire to continency, and even to perpetual continency, and thereby strive to attain to true perfection.

Not a few of Count Tolstoy's critics, particularly his clerical critics, have severely attacked him for having dared to propose Christ's ideal of chastity for our guidance in life. They have argued as if he had insisted on the obligatory fulfilment of an ideal, that is, as if he had required that all men should be celibates. They have further proposed by way of objection a most ill-placed and irrelevant question as to the consequence of the universal adoption of his doctrines, which, as they assert, would simply be the disappearance of the human race. And with what propriety can such a question be put whilst the world is still the slave of sensual passion? Why not defer it till men have learned to practise such restraint that they threaten the continuance of their race? There is, of course, no occasion to raise the question, as there is no reason to suppose that the time is near at hand when "all men shall receive this saying."

But Count Tolstoy is throughout perfectly logical. He justly remarks that when people shall have attained to the full Christian ideal, they will have no longer anything to live for.

Moreover, his critics forget that he who aspires to complete chastity, and attains it, will undoubtedly experience the highest moral satisfaction.

But if we need a proof that Count Tolstoy does not preach celibacy, but only instances complete continency as a necessary guidance in life, and an unattainable ideal, we may refer to his "Post-prefatory

Remarks," where he writes, "Chastity is not a rule, or an instruction, but an ideal, or rather one of its conditions. But an ideal is only an ideal so long as its existence is possible but in idea, in thought, when it is represented as being attainable only in the infinite, and consequently our approach towards it is also infinite."

The consequences arising from these two different views of marriage are so numerous and so varied that it would need a whole volume to enumerate them. I shall content myself with one that is most evident. It is counted almost a disgrace to a girl if she remains a maid. We have, it is true, done our little best to mitigate the unnatural harshness of this general opinion by calling them "the brides of Christ." But when we take a healthier view of marriage and chastity, it will be to the virgin that we shall give the place of honour. And at the same time coquetry, which has now become an instinct with women, will cease. Excessive luxury in dress and the ordering of our houses will no longer be the rule, and thereby a complete change will be effected in the constitution of society. But, as Posdniescheff says, "this change will only come when women count virginity to be their highest honour, instead of regarding it, as they now do, as a humiliation and a disgrace."

And this change in our view of marriage and virginity will bring a change in our systems of education. To what end do we now train our daughters? To lay themselves out from their earliest years with the single purpose of marrying, in our false sense of the word. Almost before she can walk, a girl will already have learned to dawdle and grimace before a looking-glass.

The best instruction we can give is by example. What example can contemporary family life give young persons, and what a healthy example it might give them, if we would but regard marriage from Count Tolstoy's point of view.

Whilst marriage, as we now understand it, is considered to be perfection, the slightest departure from such perfection is an act of depravity. And this is the reason why depravity reigns supreme in Europe.

Remember what Posdniescheff says of his first fall, of the lives young people lead before marriage, and how intrigues with married women are thought to be the "right thing," and bring with them no shame.

The significance of the ideal he proposes for our acceptance as a guidance to us in life is admirably set forth by Count Tolstoy in his "Post-prefatory Remarks."

He first points out the distinctive superiority of the Christian religion over all other religions. It consists in this, that Christ in Himself presented the ideal of love, one of the conditions of which is chastity, whilst other religions give only rules and instructions. In the first, there is an inward spiritual side, but in the last all is outward, and not seldom without any moral basis; as, for example, Mahomet's precept concerning frequent daily ablutions.

Later on, he compares this ideal with the compass, and declares that contemporary society, in ceasing to reverence virginity, has acted like a crew of navigators who wantonly throw their compass overboard.

He further observes that, the more widely immorality is spread, the greater is our need of a sure guidance, and the more dangerous it is to ignore that which of all things is most indispensable.

Finally, he sums up the whole matter in the following happy illustration :—

"People tell us that man is weak, and that the task we give him should be within his strength. This is exactly the same as if I were to say, My hands are weak, and I am unable to draw a line that shall be straight, that is, the shortest possible line between two points. And so, to make it easier, I take as my model a crooked or broken line, all the while wishing to draw a perfectly straight line.

"The weaker my hands, the more I stand in need of a perfect model."

IV.

WHAT, THEN, ARE WE TO DO?

THIS question, I presume, will already have been asked by my readers. And, in truth, how are we to struggle against an evil that is the growth of ages? How can we extirpate an evil that has spread over the whole civilised world? And what remedy can we propose to raise women from their humiliating position, and to counteract the extravagant luxury of modern society?

Even if we find individual persons and families who are imbued with the ideas of Count Tolstoy, they will only prove rare exceptions, and the evil will continue to flourish as before. Let us suppose that the daughters of these families voluntarily choose a life of virginity. The evil is not thereby eradicated. For the life, pleasures, and pursuits of society, beginning with the highest works of art, as Posdniescheff says, down to the trumpery picture on a match-box are so constituted as to excite and foster man's sensual passion, and this order of things would still remain the same. And it is impossible to admit that people knew nothing of the evil till recently, or could not have prevented its continual spread when once they knew of it.

The principal thing is to recognise that the evil exists, and to loathe it : what we have to do will then become plain. Nay more, no hindrances or obstacles will have force to stop mankind in their efforts to wipe it from off the face of the earth. For this reason, the first who comes to the front and sets the example must have a great influence on the rest of men, and will give a powerful incentive to the movement.

It is only women, I repeat, who can uproot this evil. Men are corrupted to such an extent in all that concerns the control of their passions, that they are absolutely incapacitated from struggling against sensualism. The doctors are right when they assert that the sensual instinct exists in man, but they are wrong when they declare it to be normal. We must learn to look upon it as a malady, and to treat it as such.

If only women will acknowledge the evil, and open their hearts to a feeling of deep pity for posterity, they will of themselves begin the work, and will soon find the means of bringing their work to a successful issue.

I could mention many such means, but it might easily happen that, under certain circumstances, the most rational of these means would turn out to be superfluous, and the least promising prove to be the best and the most necessary.

On the one hand, you must act; on the other hand, you must protest. You can easily influence fathers, husbands, brothers, and sons, so that they shall submit their lives to the law of reason. And it often happens that individual efforts prove more fruitful than any legislative exactment.

It is very possible that the present generation will not abate in one iota its abandonment to sensual pleasure; and it is plain that it cannot retrieve its past.

Our greatest care should be for our children and for posterity. It is, therefore, in the family that the most effectual stand can be made against the evil. Only in the family circle can the reaction take its rise. And in this reaction, time and education are the leading factors, motherly love and endurance the two chief agents.

In educating our children we must mainly direct our attention to the abatement and gradual extinction of sensual passion, and to fill their minds with a lively fear and horror of its pernicious nature. It is so strong and insidious that, in spite of ourselves, it will make its power felt whilst they are still too young to marry. But we have no need to despair of success. Though our medical men and teachers in general interest themselves but little in this question, every mother knows how the moral growth of a child may be injured by excessive food, unwise tenderness, the example of its elders, the atmosphere of home life, and the lack of that physical bodily exercise which is so necessary to its healthy development.

Together with the regeneration of family life an equally desirable change will little by little be effected in the life of the outer world. The general tone of society will become purer. Where there is no demand there will be no supply. To give but one instance, our so-called humorous publications will no longer find it profitable to publish cartoons of a questionable char-

acter, and our popular literature will cease
to pander to vice.

With you and in France the free every
healthy movement is sure to spread quickly,
and is certain to meet with ready sympathy.
It is in this belief that I have ventured to
address this letter to you, and endeavoured
to explain to you the character and ten-
dencies of the social reform advocated by
Count Tolstoy. We have long been accustomed to look to Western Europe for
example and encouragement. I would fain
hope that, on the present occasion, you will
not refuse to extend your support to that
reform, and thereby prove that, unlike the
larger majority of his fellow-countrymen,
you are able and willing to value at its true
worth the high teaching of the greatest of
our writers.

Printed by BALLANTYNE, HANSON & CO.
Edinburgh and London

Telegraphic Address:
Sunlocks, London.

21 BEDFORD STREET, W.C.

A LIST OF

MR WILLIAM HEINEMANN'S

PUBLICATIONS

AND

FORTHCOMING WORKS

The Books mentioned in this List can be obtained to order by any Bookseller if not in stock, or will be sent by the Publisher post free on receipt of price.

TWENTY-FIVE YEARS IN THE SECRET SERVICE.

THE RECOLLECTIONS OF A SPY.

BY

MAJOR LE CARON.

In One Volume, 8vo. With Portraits and Facsimiles. Price 14*s.*

ALFRED, LORD TENNYSON:

A STUDY OF HIS LIFE AND WORK.

BY

ARTHUR WAUGH, B.A. Oxon.

WITH TWENTY-ONE ILLUSTRATIONS,

From Photographs Specially Taken for this Work, and Five Portraits.

Second Edition, Revised. In One Volume, Demy 8vo, 10*s.* 6*d.*

STUDIES OF RELIGIOUS HISTORY.

BY

ERNEST RENAN,

LATE OF THE FRENCH ACADEMY

In One Volume, 8vo, 7s. 6d.

QUEEN JOANNA I.

OF NAPLES, SICILY, AND JERUSALEM;

COUNTESS OF PROVENCE FORCALQUIER, AND PIEDMONT.

AN ESSAY ON HER TIMES.

BY

ST. CLAIR BADDELEY.

Imperial 8vo. With Numerous Illustrations, 16*s.*

THE GREAT WAR OF 189-.

A FORECAST.

BY

**REAR-ADMIRAL COLOMB, COL. MAURICE, R.A.,
CAPTAIN MAUDE, ARCHIBALD FORBES,
CHARLES LOWE, D. CHRISTIE MURRAY,
and F. SCUDAMORE.**

In One Volume, large 8vo.   With Numerous Illustrations, 12s. 6d.

VICTORIA:

QUEEN AND EMPRESS.

BY

JOHN CORDY JEAFFRESON,

Author of "The Real Lord Byron," etc.

In Two Volumes, 8vo.   With Portraits.   [*In the Press.*

SONGS ON STONE.

BY

J. McNEILL WHISTLER.

A series of lithographic drawings in colour, by Mr. WHISTLER, will appear from time to time in parts, under the above title. Each containing four plates. The first issue of 200 copies will be sold at Two Guineas net per part, by Subscription for the Series only.

There will also be issued 50 copies on Japanese paper signed by the artist, each Five Guineas net.

RECOLLECTIONS OF
COUNT LEO NICHOLAEVITCH TOLSTOI.

BY

C. A. BEHRS,

TRANSLATED FROM THE RUSSIAN BY

PROFESSOR C. E. TURNER.

In One Volume, Crown 8vo.

The Great Educators.

A Series of Volumes by Eminent Writers, presenting in their entirety "A Biographical History of Education."

The Times.—"A Series of Monographs on 'The Great Educators' should prove of service to all who concern themselves with the history, theory, and practice of education."

The Speaker.—"There is a promising sound about the title of Mr. Heinemann's new series, 'The Great Educators.' It should help to allay the hunger and thirst for knowledge and culture of the vast multitude of young men and maidens which our educational system turns out yearly, provided at least with an appetite for instruction."

Each subject will form a complete volume, crown 8vo, 5*s.*

Now ready.

ARISTOTLE, and the Ancient Educational Ideals.
THOMAS DAVIDSON, M.A., LL.D.
The Times.—"A very readable sketch of a very interesting subject."

LOYOLA, and the Educational System of the Jesuits. By
Rev. THOMAS HUGHES, S.J.
Saturday Review.—"Full of valuable information. . . . . If a schoolmaster would learn how the education of the young can be carried on so as to confer real dignity on those engaged in it, we recommend him to read Mr. Hughes' book."

ALCUIN, and the Rise of the Christian Schools. By
Professor ANDREW F. WEST, Ph.D.

In preparation.

ABELARD, and the Origin and Early History of Universities. By JULES GABRIEL COMPAYRE, Professor in the Faculty of Toulouse.

ROUSSEAU; or, Education according to Nature.

HERBART; or, Modern German Education.

PESTALOZZI; or, the Friend and Student of Children.

FROEBEL. By H. COURTHOPE BOWEN, M.A.

HORACE MANN, and Public Education in the United States. By NICHOLAS MURRAY BUTLER, Ph.D.

BELL, LANCASTER, and ARNOLD; or, the English Education of To-Day. By J. G. FITCH, LL.D., Her Majesty's Inspector of Schools.

Others to follow.

Fiction.

In Three Volumes.

THE HEAD OF THE FIRM. By Mrs. RIDDELL, Author of " George Geith," " Maxwell Drewett," &c. *[Just ready.*

THE TOWER OF TADDEO. A Novel. By OUIDA, Author of "Two Little Wooden Shoes," &c. *[Just ready.*

KITTY'S FATHER. By FRANK BARRETT. Author of " Lieutenant Barnabas," &c. *[In November.*

CHILDREN OF THE GHETTO. By I. ZANGWILL, Author of " The Old Maids' Club," &c. *[Just ready.*

THE COUNTESS RADNA. By W. E. NORRIS, Author of " Matrimony," &c. *[In January.*

ORIOLE'S DAUGHTER. A Novel. By JESSIE FOTHERGILL, Author of " The First Violin," &c. *[In February.*

THE LAST SENTENCE. By MAXWELL GRAY, Author of " The Silence of Dean Maitland," &c. *[In March.*

In Two Volumes.

WOMAN AND THE MAN. A Love Story. By ROBERT BUCHANAN, Author of " Come Live with Me and be My Love," " The Moment After," "The Coming Terror," &c. *[In preparation.*

A KNIGHT OF THE WHITE FEATHER. By " TASMA,, Author of "The Penance of Portia James," "Uncle Piper of Piper' Hill," &c. *[Just ready.*

A LITTLE MINX. By ADA CAMBRIDGE, Author of "A Marked Man," "The Three Miss Kings," &c. *[In the Press.*

In One Volume.

THE NAULAHKA. A Tale of West and East. By RUDYARD KIPLING and WOLCOTT BALESTIER. Crown 8vo, cloth, 6s. Second Edition. *[Just ready.*

THE SECRET OF NARCISSE. By EDMUND GOSSE. Crown 8vo, 5s. *[Just ready.*

AVENGED ON SOCIETY. By H. F. WOOD, Author of " The Englishman of the Rue Cain," " The Passenger from Scotland Yard." Crown 8vo. *[In the Press.*

THE DOMINANT SEVENTH. A Musical Story. By KATE ELIZABETH CLARKE. Crown 8vo, cloth, 5s. *Speaker.*—" A very romantic story."

PASSION THE PLAYTHING. A Novel. By R. MURRAY GILCHRIST. Crown 8vo, cloth, 6s. *Athenæum.*—" This well-written story must be read to be appreciated."

Popular 3s. 6d. Novels.

NOR WIFE, NOR MAID. By Mrs. HUNGERFORD, Author of "Molly Bawn," &c.

Queen.—"It has all the characteristics of the writer's work, and greater emotional depth than most of its predecessors."
Scotsman.—"Delightful reading, supremely interesting.'

MAMMON. A Novel. By Mrs. ALEXANDER, Author of "The Wooing O't," &c.

Scotsman.—"The present work is not behind any of its predecessors. 'Mammon' is a healthy story, and as it has been thoughtfully written it has the merit of creating thought in its readers."

DAUGHTERS OF MEN. By HANNAH LYNCH, Author of "The Prince of the Glades," &c.

Daily Telegraph.—"Singularly clever and fascinating."
Academy.—"One of the cleverest, if not also the pleasantest, stories that have appeared for a long time."

A ROMANCE OF THE CAPE FRONTIER. By BERTRAM MITFORD, Author of "Through the Zulu Country," &c.

Observer.—"This is a rattling tale, genial, healthy, and spirited."

'TWEEN SNOW AND FIRE. A Tale of the Kafir War of 1877. By BERTRAM MITFORD.

THE MASTER OF THE MAGICIANS. By ELIZABETH STUART PHELPS and HERBERT D. WARD.

Athenæum.—"A thrilling story."

THE AVERAGE WOMAN. By WOLCOTT BALESTIER. With an Introduction by HENRY JAMES.

THE ATTACK ON THE MILL and Other Sketches of War. By EMILE ZOLA. With an essay on the short stories of M. Zola by Edmund Gosse.

DUST. By BJÖRNSTJERNE BJÖRNSON. Translated from the Norwegian. *[In the Press.*

MADEMOISELLE MISS and Other Stories. By HENRY HARLAND, Author of "Mea Culpa," &c. *[In the Press.*

LOS CERRITOS. A Romance of the Modern Time. By GERTRUDE FRANKLIN ATHERTON, Author of "Hermia Suydam," and "What Dreams may Come."

Athenæum.—"Full of fresh fancies and suggestions. Told with strength and delicacy. A decidedly charming romance."

A MODERN MARRIAGE. By the Marquise CLARA LANZA.

Queen.—"A powerful story, dramatically and consistently carried out."
Black and White.—"A decidedly clever book."

Popular 3s. 6d. Novels.

CAPT'N DAVY'S HONEYMOON, The Blind Mother, and The Last Confession. By HALL CAINE, Author of "The Bondman," "The Scapegoat," &c.

THE SCAPEGOAT. By HALL CAINE, Author of "The Bondman," &c.

Mr. Gladstone writes:—"I congratulate you upon 'The Scapegoat' as a work of art, and especially upon the noble and skilfully drawn character of Israel."

Times.—"In our judgment it excels in dramatic force all his previous efforts. For grace and touching pathos Naomi is a character which any romancist in the world might be proud to have created."

THE BONDMAN. A New Saga. By HALL CAINE. Twentieth Thousand.

Mr. Gladstone.—"'The Bondman' is a work of which I recognise the freshness, vigour, and sustained interest no less than its integrity of aim."

Standard.—"Its argument is grand, and it is sustained with a power that is almost marvellous."

DESPERATE REMEDIES. By THOMAS HARDY, Author of "Tess of the D'Urbervilles," &c.

Saturday Review.—"A remarkable story worked out with abundant skill."

A MARKED MAN: Some Episodes in his Life. By ADA CAMBRIDGE, Author of "Two Years' Time," "A Mere Chance," &c.

Morning Post.—"A depth of feeling, a knowledge of the human heart, and an amount of tact that one rarely finds. Should take a prominent place among the novels of the season."

THE THREE MISS KINGS. By ADA CAMBRIDGE, Author of "A Marked Man."

Athenæum.—"A charming study of character. The love stories are excellent, and the author is happy in tender situations."

NOT ALL IN VAIN. By ADA CAMBRIDGE, Author of "A Marked Man," "The Three Miss Kings," &c.

Guardian.—"A clever and absorbing story."

Queen.—"All that remains to be said is 'read the book.'"

UNCLE PIPER OF PIPER'S HILL. By TASMA. New Popular Edition.

Guardian.—"Every page of it contains good wholesome food, which demands and repays digestion. The tale itself is thoroughly charming, and all the characters are delightfully drawn. We strongly recommend all lovers of wholesome novels to make acquaintance with it themselves, and are much mistaken if they do not heartily thank us for the introduction."

IN THE VALLEY. By HAROLD FREDERIC, Author of "The Lawton Girl," "Seth's Brother's Wife," &c. With Illustrations.

Times.—"The literary value of the book is high; the author's studies of bygone life presenting a life-like picture."

PRETTY MISS SMITH. By FLORENCE WARDEN, Author of "The House on the Marsh," "A Witch of the Hills," &c.

Punch.—"Since Miss Florence Warden's 'House on the Marsh,' I have not read a more exciting tale."

Heinemann's International Library.

EDITED BY EDMUND GOSSE.

New Review.—" If you have any pernicious remnants of literary chauvinism I hope it will not survive the series of foreign classics of which Mr. William Heinemann, aided by Mr. Edmund Gosse, is publishing translations to the great contentment of all lovers of literature."

Times.—"A venture which deserves encouragement."

Each Volume has an Introduction specially written by the Editor.

Price, in paper covers, 2s. 6d. each, or cloth, 3s. 6d.

IN GOD'S WAY. From the Norwegian of BJÖRNSTJERNE BJÖRNSON.

Athenæum.—" Without doubt the most important and the most interesting work published during the twelve months."

PIERRE AND JEAN. From the French of GUY DE MAUPASSANT.

Pall Mall Gazette.—" So fine and faultless, so perfectly balanced, so steadily progressive, so clear and simple and satisfying. It is admirable from beginning to end."

Athenæum.—" Ranks amongst the best gems of modern French fiction."

THE CHIEF JUSTICE. From the German of KARL EMIL FRANZOS, Author of " For the Right," &c.

New Review.—" Few novels of recent times have a more sustained and vivid human interest."

WORK WHILE YE HAVE THE LIGHT. From the Russian of Count LYOF TOLSTOY.

Manchester Guardian.—" Readable and well translated ; full of high and noble feeling."

FANTASY. From the Italian of MATILDE SERAO.

Scottish Leader.—" The book is full of a glowing and living realism. . . . . There is nothing like ' Fantasy ' in modern literature."

FROTH. From the Spanish of Don ARMANDO PALACIO-VALDÉS.

Daily Telegraph.—" Vigorous and powerful in the highest degree. It abounds in forcible delineation of character, and describes scenes with rare and graphic strength."

FOOTSTEPS OF FATE. From the Dutch of LOUIS COUPERUS.

Gentlewoman.—" The consummate art of the writer prevents this tragedy from sinking to melodrama. Not a single situation is forced or a circumstance exaggerated."

PEPITA JIMÉNEZ. From the Spanish of JUAN VALERA.

New Review (Mr. George Saintsbury) :—"There is no doubt at all that it is one of the best stories that have appeared in any country in Europe for the last twenty years."

THE COMMODORE'S DAUGHTERS. From the Norwegian of JONAS LIE.

Athenæum.—" Everything that Jonas Lie writes is attractive and pleasant ; the plot of deeply human interest, and the art noble."

THE HERITAGE OF THE KURTS. From the Norwegian of BJÖRNSTJERNE BJÖRNSON.

National Observer.—" It is a book to read and a book to think about, for, incontestably, it is the work of a man of genius."

In the Press.

LOU. From the German of BARON F. v. ROBERTS.

DONA LUZ. From the Spanish of JUAN VALERA.

WITHOUT DOGMA. From the Polish of H. SIENKIEWICZ.

THE COMING TERROR. And other Essays and Letters. By ROBERT BUCHANAN. Second Edition. Demy 8vo, cloth, 12s. 6d.

ARABIC AUTHORS: A Manual of Arabian History and Literature. By F. F. ARBUTHNOT, M.R.A.S., Author of " Early Ideas," "Persian Portraits," &c. 8vo, cloth, 10s.

THE LABOUR MOVEMENT IN AMERICA. By RICHARD T. ELY, Ph.D., Associate in Political Economy, Johns Hopkins University. Crown 8vo, cloth, 5s.

THE LITTLE MANX NATION. (Lectures delivered at the Royal Institution, 1891.) By HALL CAINE, Author of "The Bondman," "The Scapegoat," &c. Crown 8vo, cloth, 3s. 6d.; paper, 2s. 6d.

NOTES FOR THE NILE. Together with a Metrical Rendering of the Hymns of Ancient Egypt and of the Precepts of Ptahhotep (the oldest book in the world). By HARDWICKE D. RAWNSLEY, M.A. 16mo, cloth, 5s.

DENMARK: Its History, Topography, Language, Literature, Fine Arts, Social Life, and Finance. Edited by H. WEITEMEYER. Demy 8vo, cloth, with Map, 12s. 6d.

  *** *Dedicated, by permission, to H.R.H. the Princess of Wales.* ·

IMPERIAL GERMANY. A Critical Study of Fact and Character. By SIDNEY WHITMAN. New Edition, Revised and Enlarged. Crown 8vo, cloth 2s. 6d.; paper, 2s.

THE CANADIAN GUIDE-BOOK. Part I. The Tourist's and Sportsman's Guide to Eastern Canada and Newfoundland, including full descriptions of Routes, Cities, Points of Interest, Summer Resorts, Fishing Places, &c., in Eastern Ontario, The Muskoka District, The St. Lawrence Region, The Lake St. John Country, The Maritime Provinces, Prince Edward Island, and Newfoundland. With an Appendix giving Fish and Game Laws, and Official Lists of Trout and Salmon Rivers and their Lessees. By CHARLES G. D. ROBERTS, Professor of English Literature in King's College, Windsor, N.S. With Maps and many Illustrations. Crown 8vo. limp cloth, 6s.

Part II. **WESTERN CANADA.** Including the Peninsula and Northern Regions of Ontario, the Canadian Shores of the Great Lakes, the Lake of the Woods Region, Manitoba and "The Great North-West," The Canadian Rocky Mountains and National Park, British Columbia, and Vancouver Island. By ERNEST INGERSOLL. With Maps and many Illustrations. Crown 8vo, limp cloth, 6s.

THE GENESIS OF THE UNITED STATES. A Narrative of the Movement in England, 1605-1616, which resulted in the Plantation of North America by Englishmen, disclosing the Contest between England and Spain for the Possession of the Soil now occupied by the United States of America; set forth through a series of Historical Manuscripts now first printed, together with a Re-issue of Rare Contemporaneous Tracts, accompanied by Bibliographical Memoranda, Notes, and Brief Biographies. Collected, Arranged, and Edited by ALEXANDER BROWN, F.R.H.S. With 100 Portraits, Maps, and Plans. In two volumes. Royal 8vo, buckram, £3 13s. 6d.

THE ARBITRATOR'S MANUAL. Under the London Chamber of Arbitration. Being a Practical Treatise on the Power and Duties of an Arbitrator, with the Rules and Procedure of the Court of Arbitration, and the Forms. By JOSEPH SEYMOUR SALAMAN, Author of "Trade Marks," etc. Fcap. 8vo. 3s. 6d.

THE GENTLE ART OF MAKING ENEMIES. As pleasingly exemplified in many instances, wherein the serious ones of this earth, carefully exasperated, have been prettily spurred on to indiscretions and unseemliness, while overcome by an undue sense of right. By J. M'NEIL WHISTLER. *A New Edition.* Pott 4to, half cloth, 10s. 6d.
[Just ready.

THE JEW AT HOME. Impressions of a Summer and Autumn Spent with Him in Austria and Russia. By JOSEPH PENNELL. With Illustrations by the Author. 4to, cloth, 5s. *[Just ready.*

THE NEW EXODUS. A Study of Israel in Russia. By HAROLD FREDERIC. Demy 8vo, Illustrated. 16s. *[Just ready.*

THE REALM OF THE HABSBURGS. By SIDNEY WHITMAN, Author of "Imperial Germany." In One Volume. Crown 8vo, 7s. 6d.

PRINCE BISMARCK. An Historical Biography. By CHARLES LOWE, M.A. With Portraits. Crown 8vo, 6s. *[Just ready.*

THE WORKS OF HEINRICH HEINE. Translated by CHARLES GODFREY LELAND, M.A., F.R.L.S. (Hans Breitmann.) Crown 8vo, cloth, 5s. per Volume.

I. FLORENTINE NIGHTS, SCHNABELEWOPSKI, THE RABBI OF BACHARACH, and SHAKESPEARE'S MAIDENS AND WOMEN. *[Ready.*

Times.—"We can recommend no better medium for making acquaintance at first hand with 'the German Aristophanes' than the works of Heinrich Heine, translated by Charles Godfrey Leland. Mr. Leland manages pretty successfully to preserve the easy grace of the original."

II., III. PICTURES OF TRAVEL. 1823-1828. In Two Volumes. *[Ready.*

Daily Chronicle.—"Mr. Leland's translation of 'The Pictures of Travel' is one of the acknowledged literary feats of the age. As a traveller Heine is delicious beyond description, and a volume which includes the magnificent Lucca series, the North Sea, the memorable Hartz wanderings, must needs possess an everlasting charm."

IV. THE BOOK OF SONGS. *[In the Press.*

V., VI. GERMANY. In Two Volumes. *[Ready.*

Daily Telegraph.—"Mr. Leland has done his translation in able and scholarly fashion."

VII., VIII. FRENCH AFFAIRS. In Two Volumes.
[In the Press.

IX. THE SALON. *[In preparation.*

⁎⁎ *Large Paper Edition, limited to 100 Numbered Copies. Particulars on application.*

LIFE OF HEINRICH HEINE. By RICHARD GARNETT, LL.D. With Portrait. Crown 8vo (uniform with the translation of Heine's Works). *[In preparation.*

LITTLE JOHANNES. By FREDERICK VAN EEDEN. Translated from the Dutch by CLARA BELL. With an Introduction by ANDREW LANG. Illustrated. [*In preparation.*
*** *Also a Large Paper Edition.*

THE SPEECH OF MONKEYS. By Professor R. L. GARNER. Crown 8vo, 7s. 6d. [*Just ready.*

THE OLD MAIDS' CLUB. By I. ZANGWILL, Author of "The Bachelors' Club." Illustrated by F. H. TOWNSEND. Crown 8vo, cloth, 3s. 6d.

WOMAN—THROUGH A MAN'S EYEGLASS. By MALCOLM C. SALAMAN. With Illustrations by DUDLEY HARDY. Crown 8vo, cloth, 3s. 6d.

GIRLS AND WOMEN. By E. CHESTER. Pott 8vo, cloth, 2s. 6d., or gilt extra, 3s. 6d.

GOSSIP IN A LIBRARY. By EDMUND GOSSE, Author of "Northern Studies," &c. Second Edition. Crown 8vo, buckram, gilt top, 7s. 6d.
*** *Large Paper Edition, limited to 100 Numbered Copies, 25s. net.*

THE LIFE OF HENRIK IBSEN. By HENRIK JÆGER. Translated by CLARA BELL. With the Verse done into English from the Norwegian Original by EDMUND GOSSE. Crown 8vo, cloth, 6s.

DE QUINCEY MEMORIALS. Being Letters and other Records here first Published, with Communications from COLERIDGE, The WORDSWORTHS, HANNAH MORE, PROFESSOR WILSON and others. Edited, with Introduction, Notes, and Narrative, by ALEXANDER H. JAPP, LL.D. F.R.S.E. In two volumes, demy 8vo, cloth, with portraits, 30s. net.

THE POSTHUMOUS WORKS OF THOMAS DE QUINCEY. Edited with Introduction and Notes from the Author's Original MSS., by ALEXANDER H. JAPP, LL.D, F.R.S.E., &c. Crown 8vo, cloth, 6s. each.

I. SUSPIRIA DE PROFUNDIS. With other Essays.

II. CONVERSATION AND COLERIDGE. With other Essays. [*In preparation.*

THE WORD OF THE LORD UPON THE WATERS Sermons read by His Imperial Majesty the Emperor of Germany, while at Sea on his Voyages to the Land of the Midnight Sun. Composed by Dr. RICHTER, Army Chaplain, and Translated from the German by JOHN R. MCILRAITH. 4to, cloth, 2s. 6d.

THE HOURS OF RAPHAEL, IN OUTLINE. Together with the Ceiling of the Hall where they were originally painted. By MARY E. WILLIAMS. Folio, cloth, £2 2s. net.

THE PASSION PLAY AT OBERAMMERGAU, 1890. By F. W. FARRAR, D.D., F.R.S., Archdeacon and Canon of Westminster, &c. &c. 4to, cloth, 2s. 6d.

THE GARDEN'S STORY; or, Pleasures and Trials of an Amateur Gardener. By G. H. ELLWANGER. With an Introduction by the Rev. C. WOLLEY DOD. 12mo, cloth, with Illustrations, 5s.

IDLE MUSINGS: Essays in Social Mosaic. By E. CONDER GRAY, Author of "Wise Words and Loving Deeds," &c. &c. Crown 8vo, cloth, 6s.

The Crown Copyright Series.

Mr. HEINEMANN has made arrangements with a number of the FIRST AND MOST POPULAR ENGLISH, AMERICAN, and COLONIAL AUTHORS which will enable him to issue a series of NEW AND ORIGINAL WORKS, to be known as THE CROWN COPYRIGHT SERIES, complete in One Volume, at a uniform price of FIVE SHILLINGS EACH. These Novels will not pass through an Expensive Two or Three Volume Edition, but they will be obtainable at the CIRCULATING LIBRARIES, as well as at all Booksellers' and Bookstalls.

ACCORDING TO ST. JOHN. By AMÉLIE RIVES, Author of "The Quick or the Dead."

Scotsman.—"The literary work is highly artistic. . . . . It has beauty and brightness, and a kind of fascination which carries the reader on till he has read to the last page."

THE PENANCE OF PORTIA JAMES. By TASMA, Author of "Uncle Piper of Piper's Hill," &c.

Athenæum.—"A powerful novel."
Daily Chronicle.—"Captivating and yet tantalising, this story is far above the average."
Vanity Fair.—"A very interesting story, morally sound, and flavoured throughout with ease of diction and lack of strain."

INCONSEQUENT LIVES. A Village Chronicle, shewing how certain folk set out for El Dorado ; what they attempted ; and what they attained. By J. H. PEARCE, Author of "Esther Pentreath," &c.

Saturday Review.—"A vivid picture of the life of Cornish fisher-folk. It is unquestionably interesting."
Literary World.—"Powerful and pathetic . . . . from first to last it is profoundly interesting. It is long since we read a story revealing power of so high an order, marked by such evident carefulness of workmanship, such skill in the powerful and yet temperate presentation of passion, and in the sternly realistic yet delicate treatment of difficult situations."

A QUESTION OF TASTE. By MAARTEN MAARTENS, Author of "An Old Maid's Love," &c.

National Observer.—"There is more than cleverness ; there is original talent, and a good deal of humanity besides."

COME LIVE WITH ME AND BE MY LOVE. By ROBERT BUCHANAN, Author of "The Moment After," "The Coming Terror," &c.

Globe.—"Will be found eminently readable."
Daily Telegraph.—"We will conclude this brief notice by expressing our cordial admiration of the skill displayed in its construction, and the genial humanity that has inspired its author in the shaping and vitalising of the individuals created by his fertile imagination."

VANITAS. By VERNON LEE, Author of "Hauntings," &c.

THE O'CONNORS OF BALLINAHINCH. By Mrs. HUNGERFORD, Author of "Molly Bawn," &c. [*In the Press.*

A BATTLE AND A BOY. By BLANCHE WILLIS HOWARD, Author of "Guenn," &c. [*In preparation.*

www.ingramcontent.com/pod-product-compliance
Lightning Source LLC
Chambersburg PA
CBHW020851270326
41928CB00006B/657